OLF
ıard F.
ler, a p --
tyranny

ADOLF HITLER
A Portrait in Tyranny

Other Books by the Author

Matthew Henson, Black Explorer
How to Leave Home—and Make Everybody Like It
Pasteur and the Invisible Giants
Amnesty: The American Puzzle
Gun Control: A Decision for Americans
Child Abuse
The Bermuda Triangle and Other Mysteries of Nature
A Lion in the Sun: The Rise and Fall of the British Empire
Inventors for Medicine
Legal Action: A Layman's Guide

ADOLF HITLER

A Portrait in Tyranny

Edward F. Dolan, Jr.

Illustrated with photographs

DODD, MEAD & COMPANY
New York

Passages from *Mein Kampf* by Adolf Hitler, translated by Ralph Manheim. Copyright 1943 and © renewed 1971 by Houghton Mifflin Company. Reprinted by permission of Houghton Mifflin Company and Hutchinson General Books Limited.

Library of Congress Cataloging in Publication Data

Dolan, Edward F., date
    Adolf Hitler, a portrait in tyranny.

    Bibliography: p.
    Includes index.
    Summary: A biography of Adolf Hitler from his youth
to his self-destruction in a Berlin bunker.
    1. Hitler, Adolf, 1889–1945—Juvenile literature.
    2. Heads of state—Germany—Biography—Juvenile literature.
    3. Germany—Politics and government—1933–1945—Juvenile
literature. [1. Hitler, Adolf, 1889–1945.   2. Heads of
state]   I. Title.
DD247.H5D7   943.086′092′4   [B]   [92]   81–43227
ISBN 0–396–07982–2   AACR2

For Dick and Alla Crone,
good friends

CONTENTS

Illustrations following page 136

Why This Book?		*ix*
1.	The Young Years	*1*
2.	Adrift in Vienna	*14*
3.	The Crucible of War	*30*
4.	Birth of a Politician	*43*
5.	The November Adventure	*61*
6.	The Road to Berlin	*82*
7.	Power and Death	*101*
8.	Nazi Germany	*123*
9.	The Tapestry of Horror	*151*
10.	Toward a New War	*173*
11.	The World on Fire	*189*
	Recommended Reading List	*217*
	Index	*219*

Why This Book?

ADOLF HITLER came of humble beginnings. He never finished high school. He failed in his ambition to become an artist. But he understood one political art and practiced it to its fullest. With it, he first enslaved the German nation and then the bulk of Europe, and finally drove the world into the most catastrophic war it has ever known. That art was tyranny.

History has known many tyrants. They've all practiced their art in substantially the same way. Each has claimed to know what is best for the people. Each has lied shamelessly to attain his ends. Each has used the hypnotism of propaganda. Each has applied brutal force—sometimes openly, sometimes secretly—to coerce his and other nations into subservience. Each has eradicated, without mercy, those whom he has hated.

Tyranny remains with us today in many parts of the world. It—or the threat of it—will be with us for as long as there are power-hungry men in our midst.

With justice, many historians look on Hitler as the very worst of his breed. Wisdom, then, dictates that none of us ever forget what he preached, what he stood for, what he did, and how he did it. Armed with a knowledge of his life, we can more readily recognize the symptoms and the techniques of today's and tomorrow's tyranny when we see them. Recognition is always the first tool needed to resist and then overcome any evil.

To help us all—myself included—better see the dangers of the present and the future by looking at a frightening period in the past: that is the reason why this book was written.

—Edward F. Dolan, Jr.

1. THE YOUNG YEARS

AT FIRST GLANCE, Adolf Hitler's parents may have seemed to be much alike. Both came of peasant stock and Catholic families. Both were born and raised in the Waldviertal region, a forested area in southern Austria. As children, both called the village of Spital home. Their families had lived in and around the village for generations and were closely related by marriage.

But there the similarity ended. They were, first, vastly different in age; the husband was twenty-three years the wife's senior. Then there was the difference in their temperaments. For her part, Hitler's mother, Klara, was a quiet and gentle woman. She loved her son and doted on him. Hitler always remembered her death as possibly the most crushing personal blow he had ever suffered. For the rest of his life, wherever he went, he kept her photograph at his bedside.

His father, Alois, was anything but quiet and gentle. Alois, though recognized as a fair-minded man, was known among friends and family for his pride, arrogance, and quick temper. He demanded complete obedience of his children and didn't hesitate to beat them with a leather strap—or a "hippopotamus whip" as one of them called it—when they didn't jump quickly enough to his commands. For some reason, he always reserved his harshest treatment for his oldest son, Alois, Jr. The boy ran away at thirteen and never returned.

The father was also a restless man. In one four-year period, the family seemed to be moving continually while Alois, who had just retired from his job, looked for a place that pleased him. Further, he seemed to be a man who preferred the company of his tavern friends to that of his wife and children; in his retirement, it was his custom to head for the local inn each morning and not return for hours; his death came unexpectedly one morning just after he'd settled down at his favorite table and ordered his first ale of the day. Finally, he was a man of a shadowy family background. He never knew who his father was.

Alois was born in 1837 near the village of Spital. His mother was Anna Schicklgruber, a serving girl in a local household. Anna was unmarried at the time and Alois grew up with her family name. Some years later, she married a wandering miller named Johann Georg Hiedler; though he spelled his last name as he did, his relatives were also variously known as Huttler and Hitler. Local rumor had it that Johann was actually Alois' father, but this was never established as fact. Nor was another rumor ever proved out: that Alois had been fathered by a wealthy Jewish businessman of the area. Whatever the truth of the matter might have been, Alois adopted the name Hitler as an adult.

The change of name was a fateful one for his son. Historians have long wondered if the tough-talking Adolf Hitler could have gone far in politics had his last name been the comic Schicklgruber. To many, it seems unlikely. They feel that the German people simply would have been unable to take him seriously. As a case in point, they bring up the menacing chant of "Heil Hitler" that rang throughout the country at the height of his power. It was used to whip masses of Germans into a frenzy of adoration at political rallies and meetings. Could it have done so if it had been "Heil Schicklgruber"? Hardly.

Alois left home at fourteen to make his own way in the world. The boy served for a time as an apprentice shoemaker in Vienna. Then, ambitious for "something better in life," as he put it, he joined the Austrian Customs Service. Starting as a border guard, he worked his way up through the years to the position of Customs Inspector at the small city of Braunau on the Inn River just across from the German border. By now, he was in his early forties—a burly man who sported a walrus mustache and loved to be photographed in his inspector's uniform.

His professional life seems to have been a full and happy one. But not so his home life. In a period of roughly twenty years, he was widowed twice. His first wife was a frail and sickly woman; they did not get along well and she left him three years before her death. Within months of the death, he married Franziska Matzelsberger, a kitchen maid at a Braunau inn. Franziska survived the wedding by little more than a year and bore her husband two children—Alois, Jr. and a daughter, Angela—before she fell ill with the undiagnosed lung ailment that took her life. She was pregnant with Alois, Jr. at the time of the wedding.

A name that weaves its way through both marriages is that of Klara Poelzl. Born in 1860 near Spital, she was hired by Alois at age seventeen to care for his ailing first wife. Photographs of the day show Klara to have been a slim and attractive young woman with long brown hair. She was related to Johann Georg Hiedler, Alois' rumored father. If indeed he was Alois' father, then she and her employer were second cousins. Their close relationship was to cause them trouble in the near future. When Alois married for the second time, Klara was dismissed and sent to Vienna to work as a housemaid. There is no doubt that Alois had a roving eye, and Franziska apparently didn't like the way he was looking at the young girl. But then Franziska fell so ill that she could not care for her children. Klara returned and took them under her wing.

Franziska's suspicions of her husband were well founded. At the time of her death in late 1884, her housemaid was several months pregnant by Alois. A wedding date was immediately set, with Alois and Klara having to take the time to obtain a church dispensation for the marriage because of their possible close blood relationship. As soon as the dispensation was granted, they were married—on January 7, 1885. The bride was twenty-five years old, and the groom forty-eight.

The marriage seems to have been a quietly happy and contented one. Husband and wife got on well together and Alois apparently gave up his "roving eye." Friends later recalled that Klara took great pleasure in tending her home and raising her children. She obviously admired Alois and was impressed by his position as a customs inspector. In fact, she may have been a few degrees too admiring. She could never get over the habit—a leftover from her teen years as a household helper—of calling him "Uncle Alois."

Klara gave her husband six children. The first three—Gustav, Ida, and Otto—were born between early 1885 and late 1887. All three died when very young. Otto survived his birth by just a few days. Gustav and Ida were no more than toddlers when they died of diphtheria, within a month of each other.

A fourth child, a boy, was born at Braunau at 6:30 in the evening of April 20, 1889. To Klara, he seemed a sickly baby and she feared for his life. Not so a maid in the Hitler home; the woman later described the newcomer as a "healthy, lively little creature" who grew "very well." The infant was baptized Adolphus in the neighborhood Catholic church within a few days of his birth. The name was soon abbreviated to Adolf.

2.

Little is known of Adolf Hitler's earliest years. Historians feel that Klara probably spoiled him with a deluge of love and attention. She was, by nature, a loving mother (it's known that she was quite as caring for her stepchildren, Angela and Alois, Jr.) and there was, of course, the constant fear that, having already lost three little ones, she might lose this precious fourth. It seems more than likely that, for the first five to seven years of his life, the future dictator of Germany was a pampered and overly protected child.

But then he began to come into his own as an individual. In 1894, Klara gave birth to another son, Edmond; two years later, a girl, Paula, was welcomed into the family. Burdened with the care of the new arrivals, Klara had less and less time to devote to the growing Adolf. By age seven, he was running free with the children in the neighborhood.

Young Adolf proved to be an active child who enjoyed the outdoors. He liked to spend hours exploring the woods and fields near his home. He also enjoyed rough play. Two family friends later remembered how he often returned home with his clothes disheveled from some wrestling match or torn after a dash through the underbrush. They called him a "little rogue."

In his play activities, the young Hitler early showed the leadership abilities that were to take him so far in adulthood. The two family friends recalled that he was always organizing the neighborhood children into bands for raids on apple trees. His classmates in grammar school remembered him as a leader in games. His favorite game, incidentally, was cowboys and Indians. He went on enjoying it right up to his high school years.

But he also had a quiet side. Adolf Hitler early learned that he loved to read and that he had a talent for drawing. He spent long hours alone with his books and sketch pad. His favorite books were histories and the frontier tales of the American writer, James Fenimore Cooper; Cooper assuredly supplied the inspiration for many a game of cowboys and Indians. As for drawing, the boy tried his hand at everything from landscapes to designs for buildings. One day, he astonished a friend by making a highly detailed sketch of a famous Austrian castle. It was done from memory. By the time he was ten, Hitler knew that he wanted to be an artist when he grew up.

It was an ambition that remained with him into his manhood. Only once did he ever put it aside. For a time, the family moved in across the road from a Benedictine monastery and Adolf attended school there. He took the abbot as an idol, fell in love with the pageantry of the church, and decided that he must be a priest one day. The family cook later recalled that the boy would come into the kitchen and put her apron over his shoulders as if it were a priestly vestment. Then he'd climb up on a chair and deliver a long sermon. The orator who would one day hold millions of Germans under his spell was being born.

Young Hitler's leadership abilities and his talent for sketching made him popular among his friends. But he was anything but popular with his half brother. Alois, Jr. early saw in Adolf a characteristic that was to dog him throughout his life and eventually leave an imprint on world history—a temper as foul and ungovernable as their father's. As an old man in the 1940s,

The Young Years

Alois remembered how his brother could fly into a violent rage if he didn't "get his own way" and how he could become surly and angry over any trifling annoyance. It's possible that jealousy can account for some of Alois' feelings because he went on to say that Klara always "took Adolf's part" in family disputes.

But another relative—Klara's niece, Maria Schmidt—also remembered Adolf's quick temper. Klara and her children usually spent a part of their summer at the home of Maria's mother in Spital. Maria recalled that the boy Adolf seemed to live in a world of his own at times and often locked himself in his room with his books and paints. After a time, Maria and the other youngsters would make a game of throwing pebbles against the window to disturb him. Adolf would become furious, climb out the window, and chase them around the yard.

A leader. A budding artist. An avid reader. All were signs of a good mind. Adolf's intelligence was quick to show itself when he started school. The teacher at his first school—a two-room affair—recalled the boy and his half sister, Angela, as being "very alert mentally." He also called them "lively and obedient."

Hitler's father retired from the Customs Service soon after the boy started school. The family now moved a number of times while the restless Alois looked for a place that suited him, with the result that Adolf had to attend several different grade schools. He did well in all of them. His best subjects were history and art, with mathematics and grammar running a little behind them. In his last year at one school, he earned the mark of "I" in twelve subjects. It was the highest grade that a student could receive.

At last, the family settled for good on the outskirts of the city of Linz. The time came to send Adolf to high school. He was just going on twelve. He now changed, suddenly and completely. He became the worst of students.

Why?

Because father and son had gone to war with each other. By now, the boy was determined to be an artist. Alois looked on artists as disreputable creatures who did nothing but starve. He had other plans for his son. Common-sense plans. Adolf was to follow in his father's footsteps, become a respected public official, and earn a good and steady living. He was to attend a technical high school—the Realschule—in Linz. It offered courses that would prepare him for a career as a civil servant.

Follow in his father's footsteps? The ambitious young artist could not bear the idea. Years later, in his autobiography, *Mein Kampf (My Struggle)*, he described his feelings:

"I did not want to become a civil servant, no, and no again . . . I grew sick at the stomach at the thought of sitting in an office," of being "deprived of my liberty," and of never being "the master of my own time . . ."

But Hitler then wrote that his father "doubted my sanity." Alois wouldn't hear of a life in art for his son. Adolf must forget such nonsense; he must become a civil servant. Alois tried to make the boy see that the career would be an interesting one by telling him stories of his own work. Failing, he simply ordered Adolf to attend the Realschule. And so off went young Hitler to class in 1900—and to failure.

Hitler later said that he deliberately made a shambles of his high school work in the hope that his father would finally give up and let him be an artist. As an adult, he often remembered things as he wanted to remember them, and so this recollection may not be entirely true. It's just as likely that his poor performance wasn't a deliberate strategy against Alois but simply the result of stubborn rebellion.

Whatever the case, he earned the poorest of grades, with the exception of a time in his second year. He disliked most of his teachers. And many of his fellow students. The boy who had once been a leader among the children of his neighborhood now had few friends.

His dislike of the teachers was venomous. In later years, he wrote that one had been a "congenital idiot." Others, in his opinion, had been "slightly mad" and "unclean." He remembered them as "absolute tyrants" who had no sympathy for young people.

A few instructors escaped his wrath. One was Dr. Leopold Poetsch, who taught history. He had the power, Hitler said, to "transform dry historical facts into vivid reality." The boy had always loved history, but the teacher made it into "my favorite subject." Years later, the all-powerful Adolf Hitler paid a call on Dr. Poetsch, by then in retirement, and was delighted to find that the old man had long been a member of the Nazi Party.

As for the Realschule teachers themselves, their opinions of the young Hitler were nothing to write home about. One said the boy had made neither a favorable nor an unfavorable impression on him. Another thought Hitler a "gifted student" but lacking in self-control. The teacher added that he had found Hitler self-opinionated, argumentative, bad-tempered, and unable to bear school discipline. Even the admired Dr. Poetsch didn't think much of him; he gave Adolf a mark of only "fair" in history.

Hitler remained at the Realschule for almost four years, until the summer vacation of 1904. He was warned on several occasions to improve his grades or run the risk of being expelled. For some unknown reason, he did perform well in his second year. But then he fell back into his old ways. At the end of his next-to-last year, the headmaster told him that he could not return when school opened again in the fall.

The battle between father and son had begun in 1900. It raged until January 3, 1903. Early that day, as was his custom,

Alois strolled to his favorite inn. Looking pale, he sat down at his regular table and remarked that he didn't feel well. He collapsed a few minutes later and died in the arms of a friend. The cause of death was given as a lung hemorrhage. Alois was sixty-five at the time. His son was approaching his fourteenth birthday.

Though the two had long warred, Adolf wept at the sight of his dead father. Then, in the next year, he was called to the headmaster's office and told that his days at the Realschule were at an end. The news came as a shattering blow to Klara. It is true that she was proud of her son's artistic talents, but, like her husband, she wanted to see him faithfully embarked on a "practical" career in the civil service. She begged him to go to another technical school, this one at the nearby town of Steyr.

The love between mother and son had always been deep. For as long as Adolf could remember, Klara had doted on him and had tried to stand between him and his father's evil temper. Now the son could not refuse her request. Though still determined to become an artist, he dutifully set off for Steyr.

As unhappy as ever, Adolf Hitler endured his classes there for about a year. With one exception he earned grades of "adequate" and "satisfactory"; the exception was freehand drawing, in which he received an "excellent." At last, he could tolerate the school no longer. Just before receiving his certificate of graduation, he dropped out. His formal education had come to an end.

3.

Adolf Hitler had now reached sixteen. He was of medium height, a youth with a pale complexion and piercing blue eyes. He wore his hair rather long, and it was thick and unruly, wanting always to fall across his forehead. The beginnings of a moustache tried to sweep across his mouth. To one of his classmates at Steyr, he looked much like a young artist.

Once free of Steyr, he tried to live as he looked. For the next two years—a period that he later called the "happiest of my life"—he devoted himself to his dreams and his easel. He wandered through the countryside and along the Danube River each day; he painted any scene that caught his fancy. He made pencil sketches of farmhouses and inns; he put to paper the designs of buildings that crossed his mind. When weary, he lay back in the grass with a book or folded his arms beneath his head and stared at the sky and dreamed of his future in art.

At night, he often went into Linz to attend the opera or a concert, in the process becoming a lifelong admirer of the crashing music of Richard Wagner. One evening at the opera, he met a young man named August Kubizek and they became close friends. They went everywhere together, with Adolf forever pouring out his dreams and his many ideas about art and architecture while "Gustl," an accomplished pianist, tried to get in a word here and there about his ambitions to become a professional musician. A startling picture of Hitler at this time comes from Kubizek. While Hitler may have looked and acted like an artist, he didn't dress like one. The first time Kubizek saw him, the future dictator of Germany was wearing a natty overcoat and sporting a black cane with an ivory handle.

From Gustl also comes early word of a personality quirk that was to remain with his friend throughout life. Hitler had a normal young man's interest in women, but Gustl soon realized that he was abnormally shy about approaching them. The realization came when they glimpsed an attractive blonde girl strolling with her family in a Linz park. Adolf promptly fell in love. He learned where the girl lived, took to following her about at a distance, wrote love poems that were never delivered, and imagined the two of them as man and wife. The one-sided romance went on for months. An amused Gustl kept urging Hitler to walk up to his love and introduce himself. But Hitler would never go near her. Her name was Stephanie Jansten and, years later, she expressed surprise when told how much Germany's dictator had once admired her. She hadn't even been aware of his presence.

Adolf Hitler was to meet many women in his lifetime and was to have love affairs with several. So far as most women were concerned, however, unless they were simply friends or political allies, he was uncomfortable in their presence. Associates often saw him flush with embarrassment and even anger when a woman seemed to make a romantic overture. What was behind this quirk? A number of guesses have been made over the years. Some hold that he was, by nature, sexually repressed. Others contend that he wanted to see all women as being as pure as he thought his mother to be. But there is no certain answer.

Hitler also revealed other lasting traits and idiosyncracies in his teen years. He tried one cigarette and swore off smoking for the rest of his life. On leaving the school at Steyr for the last time, he celebrated by drinking too much wine; he later recalled that he passed out on a country road and was awakened the next morning by a milkmaid; he never drank again. Sometime later, he became a lifelong vegetarian. Did the refusal to smoke (in a day when smoking was not frowned upon as it is now), to drink even lightly, and to eat meat indicate a personality so repressed that it was sure to break its bonds one day and commit excesses in some other area of life? Considering Hitler's future political activities, there seems to be no other answer but "yes."

The young man may have been proud of himself as an aspiring artist, but his sisters Angela and Paula certainly weren't. It angered them—as it did friends of the family—to see him idling his days away and allowing Klara to support him on the pension left to her by his father. They felt he should get a job and were outraged when he sniffed at the idea as if everyday work was beneath him. He wanted his time to himself, he said. Wanted his freedom. The sisters glared at him in speechless exasperation. He was so—so—impractical.

But this was not entirely true. Adolf Hitler did have a practical streak in him. It told him that, really, he was just "playing" at art. If he hoped ever to compete in the art world, if he hoped ever to become a professional artist, he needed to be formally trained. He knew where he wanted to take that training—at the Academy of Arts in Vienna. Dedicated as he was to painting, he had his eye on the Academy's school, or division, of fine arts. It was one of Europe's best.

Starting at the time he left Steyr, Adolf talked constantly of the Academy, begging his mother to let him attend. And, just as constantly, Klara fended him off. The tuition costs and his board would be high and, while the family was far from penniless, money was tight. Further, she still wanted to see him obey his father's wishes and enter the safe and secure civil service. And so the issue remained unresolved until he was eighteen.

Then, once again proving that she could never refuse this cherished son a single wish, Klara relented. She nodded. Yes, Adolf could go to Vienna. Yes, he could take the Academy's entrance examination. Yes, he could enroll in the school if he passed the examination.

For Hitler, the past two years had been happy ones. But not one of their moments had been as happy as this one. The time of "playing" at art and dreaming was at an end. Now he was to begin his first real work. At last, he was actually on his way to his goal.

2. ADRIFT IN VIENNA

THE YOUNG ARTIST arrived in Vienna in October, 1907. He was thrilled to be in the great city, thrilled to be surrounded by its 2 million bustling people, its wide boulevards and great buildings, its opera house, its concert halls. But he had little time to savor them. Because he immediately ran into a shattering disappointment. He took the entrance examination to the Academy's school of fine arts, failed, and was refused admission. One word under his name in the record of the test said it all: his drawings were "unsatisfactory."

Hitler was stunned. Failure! It was a possibility that hadn't once crossed his mind. The test results, as he himself put it in *Mein Kampf*, struck him "as a bolt from the blue." But he wasn't struck speechless. He went to the Academy rector and demanded an explanation—and got one.

Patiently, the rector went over the flaws in Adolf's drawings.

Then he turned to several sketches that the young man had made of buildings. They indicated, he said, a beginning talent in architecture. The Academy maintained a school of architecture and the rector suggested that Hitler now sit for its entrance examination.

The people who have seen Hitler's early work agree that the rector had the right idea. Hitler appeared to have a flare for architectural drawing while his paintings and oils and watercolors revealed only a small talent. They seemed lifeless and stilted, with his human figures being especially poor. In his book, *The Rise and Fall of the Third Reich,* foreign correspondent William L. Shirer said that he once viewed a number of Hitler's paintings. He remarked that the human figures in them looked at times like cartoons.

The disappointed Hitler found the idea of architecture appealing, though he thought it fell far short of his original goal. But, as he wandered the streets of Vienna and tried to digest his failure and what it had done to his dreams for the future, he knew the rector's suggestion posed a problem. The Academy's school of architecture required a high school diploma for entrance. He didn't have one. He'd have to go back to Steyr. Finish his work there. Earn his graduation certificate. He couldn't stand the thought of returning to those stuffy classrooms. Nor could he bring himself to write his mother Klara of his failure. . . .

But then a letter from home reached him. It was written by his younger sister, Paula, and it drove all thoughts of his own problem from mind. The beloved Klara was desperately ill.

Actually, the news did not come as a great surprise. Early in the year, Klara had visited Dr. Edward Block, a Jewish physician in Linz, to complain of a severe pain in the chest. Dr. Block's examination revealed the presence of a large tumor in one breast. He determined that it was cancerous.

The doctor did not immediately inform Klara of the seriousness of her condition. Rather, he had called Adolf and Paula to his office. He told them that there was only one hope for saving their mother's life. Klara must agree to surgery and the breast must be removed. Dr. Block never forgot Hitler's reaction. The young man's face contorted. Tears started up in his eyes. He asked if there was no other alternative. The answer was a slow shake of the doctor's head.

Klara underwent the surgery in late January of 1907. She had then spent the rest of the year recuperating, though never recovering fully. She was still in poor health when Hitler left for Vienna in October. Loving his mother as he did, there is no doubt that he departed with a deep sense of guilt. He'd been truly faced with a dilemma. The Academy entrance exams were held only once a year. If he missed them this year, he'd have to delay the start of his studies for another twelve long months. His impatience had finally won out over his desire to stay with his mother.

Now, with the dread letter in his pocket, he rushed back to Linz. There, Paula told him how bad things were. The surgery had not been performed in time. The cancer was still present and it was spreading. Klara was undergoing a last and desperate—and horribly painful—treatment. Almost daily, a substance known as iodoform was being placed on the still open wound left by the surgery. It was a form of iodine and it seared deep into the tissue. It also affected Klara's throat, making it almost impossible for her to swallow.

During the next weeks, Adolf devoted his every waking moment to caring for and comforting his mother. We have this on the authority of Gustl Kubizek, who came often to visit the Hitler home. Gustl later recalled that his friend slept close to Klara's bedside. That he read aloud to her. That he spent long hours quietly talking with her. That he helped Paula with the cooking and the housework. He was, in a word, no longer the dreamy young artist but the worried and all-solicitous son. Kubizek said that Hitler, now always pale and drawn, couldn't endure the fact that his mother was dying. Periodically, Kubizck had to listen as Hitler raged against the ineptitude of doctors.

Klara's suffering ended just before Christmas. She died early in the morning of December 21, 1907. When Dr. Block arrived to sign the death certificate, he found the young Hitler sitting at his mother's bedside. He was holding her hand and weeping. On his lap was a last sketch that he had made of her. Dr. Block later wrote that he had seen much grief in the course of his career, but none as deep as the young Hitler's. In *Mein Kampf,* Hitler expressed his feelings of that morning in one sentence. It is one of the most striking in the entire book: "I had honored my father, but my mother I had loved."

Klara was buried alongside her husband. By early February, 1908, Hitler was ready to resume his life. Financed by a modest bequest left to him by his mother, he packed his belongings and put Linz behind him for good. He returned to Vienna.

2.

On his arrival in the city, Hitler settled into a tiny apartment near the Academy. He had decided that he couldn't bear the strain of finishing his high school work. Instead, he was determined to forget the rector's advice and try again for the school of fine arts. And so he whiled the months away until it was time for the next entrance examination. Once more, he became the "young artist," sketching and reading during the day, strolling the avenues in the evening, sipping coffee in the cafes, attending the opera or concerts whenever he felt he could afford them.

At the end of it all, there was again disappointment. This time, it was even more bitter. Before taking the examination, Hitler was made to pass a preliminary test. He had to submit a number of drawings to show that he had come nearer to the Academy's standards. The work was considered so poor that he wasn't even permitted to sit for the examination.

In the wake of this new defeat, Adolf Hitler's life took a sudden and strange turn. Though Vienna was a rich and cultured city, it was not without its seamy side—its shabby streets, its slums, its prostitutes and derelicts, its world of lost souls. Without a word even to Gustl Kubizek, Hitler left his apartment and disappeared into this world. He was to remain there for five years, a "black" period when "hunger was to be my constant companion."

Why did he do it? No one can say for certain. Perhaps, with the money left to him by Klara running out, he chose poverty rather than the humiliation of a defeated return to Linz. Perhaps he was still seeking, in a blind and pointless way, the life of an artist. Perhaps he was punishing himself for his failure. Only one thing can be said for sure: he was lost.

Whatever his reasons, Hitler now became one of Vienna's lost souls. Gone were the days of sketching and reading; he now wandered the streets or warmed himself in some doorway or public building. Gone were the nights at concerts or the opera; now he curled up on park benches for a few hours of chilled sleep or, if he had the money, got a bed in a flophouse. Gone were the cafes with their delicious pastries and coffee; now, to survive, he got into line at the charity soup kitchens that dotted the slum area. He begged for money on street corners and, when the pickings were too slim, took an occasional odd job. Once, he dug ditches for about a week. He shoveled snow in the winter. For a time, he carried baggage from a railroad station to waiting cabs. He ran errands.

Not once, though, did he look for a regular job. The deadly routine of daily work, as always, was not for him. Though lost, though his drawing materials had been pawned, he remained an artist at heart. His freedom—if the life of a street wanderer can be called freedom—meant more to him than the aches of an empty belly.

Had Hitler tried for a regular job, it is doubtful that any respectable employer would have taken a chance on him. The nattily dressed youth that Kubizek remembered—the sophisticated opera devotee with tailored overcoat and black cane—had disappeared. Hitler's clothes were now dirty and patched. He wore a long topcoat, black and shapeless, that a fellow derelict, a Jew named Josef Neumann, had given him. It had a greasy look to it, as did the bowler hat that he wore jammed down almost to his ears. He was unshaven, his face covered with a beard that never managed to be more than a stubble. His hair, uncut and unwashed, hung down over his collar.

In 1910, just as he turned twenty-one, Hitler moved into the Mannerheim, a home for destitute men. Located near the center of Vienna, it was a modern facility by the standards of the day. Able to accommodate 500 residents, it featured a kitchen that produced simple and nutritious meals. Its dormitories were divided into cubicles so that each man had a "room" to himself; each cubicle measured about seven feet long by five feet wide and contained an iron bed, a small table, a chair, and a clothes rack. There was a communal shower; the rules called for it to be used daily. For the first time in months, Hitler was clean again.

The men paid no more than a few pennies a day to live at the Mannerheim. No sooner had Hitler settled in than his fortunes took a turn for the better. He befriended a man named Reinhold Hanisch, a former servant with a goodly dash of salesmanship to him. On learning that Hitler was an aspiring artist,

Hanisch was quick to concoct a money-making scheme. He had Hitler retrieve his pawned art materials and then he sat him down at a table in the large recreation room where many of the residents spent their days. Hitler was now to sketch Vienna scenes on little postcards. Hanisch would take the finished products out on the streets and peddle them to passing tourists. The two partners would split the proceeds.

The venture proved to be a profitable one—at least, profitable enough for Hitler to go on paying his Mannerheim rent and buy some fresh clothing. Soon, he added small watercolors to his output. Hanisch sold some of the watercolors to taverns to decorate their walls. Others went to art dealers who used them to fill empty picture frames being displayed for sale. Some were bought by furniture dealers and were tacked to the backs of easy chairs; they were intended as bonuses for customers.

In *The Rise and Fall of the Third Reich*, William L. Shirer estimates that hundreds of the postcards and watercolors were sold. All were of Vienna scenes and were copied from illustrations in books and magazines. One of Hitler's greatest failings in art had always been his inability to draw anything from life.

The Hitler-Hanisch partnership lasted for several months. Then, finding that he had been cheated on a sale, Hitler broke away in a rage. It seems that he received 10 kronen as his share of the proceeds, only to learn a little later that the sale had actually been for 50 kronen. For a time afterwards, Josef Neumann, the man who had given Hitler his overcoat, acted as his salesman. And, for a time, the artist did his own selling.

At some point in his Mannerheim stay, Adolf Hitler painted several advertising posters for local merchants. One sang the praises of a product called "Teddy's Perspiration Powder." Another showed Kris Kringle holding some brightly colored Christmas candles. Still another depicted the spires of a famous

Viennese church—St. Stephen's—rising out of a mountain of soap cakes.

And so the months passed quietly for Hitler at the Mannerheim. Daily, he would take his pens and paints to his table in the recreation room. It stood in the light of a large window and it was indeed "his table." His fellow residents, awestruck by the presence of a working artist in their midst, would never think of sitting there and were quick to shoo away any newcomer who happened to eye it. For hours at a time, Hitler would remain hunched over his drawings, working slowly and carefully. But then he would relax for a while with a book or a newspaper. Or his ears would catch the talk at the nearby tables. If the conversation dealt with politics, he couldn't resist it. He'd push his materials aside. He'd fling himself into the talk and transform it into a heated debate.

Politics. It was a subject that had long interested Hitler. Now, in his young and lost manhood, it was developing into a passion that would one day make him forget his dreams of a life in art.

Where did the fascination for politics spring from? Its roots can be traced to a series of events that occurred in the years just before his birth.

3.

For more than ten centuries, from A.D. 800 onward, Austria had been a member of an alliance of German states. The alliance was originally known as the Holy Roman Empire of German States (because its first Emperor had been crowned by the Pope at Rome). Then, after Napoleon had ripped Europe apart with his wars of the early 1800s, it became the German Confederation. Consisting of some 300 states of varying size, it ranged over the face of central Europe. The largest and most powerful of the states were Austria and its ambitious neighbor to the north, Prussia.

At the time the Confederation was established, the alliance was a loosely-knit one, with each of the states being virtually independent. Prussia set out to weld them into a unified nation—Germany—that would then be under her control. But the Prussian leaders feared Austria's power and wanted to see her excluded from the planned nation. To this end, Prussia deliberately maneuvered Austria into a war, just twenty-three years before Hitler was born.

The Austro-Prussian War lasted a mere seven weeks in 1866. Fielding the most efficient army in Europe, the Prussians literally crushed their foe, slaughtering 40,000 Austrians in one battle alone. Austria was expelled from the German Confederation. The unification of Germany under the Prussian monarch, the Kaiser, began.

As for Austria, she quickly turned to Hungary, a country to her east that she had once dominated. Together, they now formed a new empire. Formally christened Austria-Hungary, it was a partnership that angered and frightened many Austrians. Why? Because Hungary was a nation of Slavic peoples— a nation not only of its own Magyars but also of Serbians, Croatians, Czechoslovakians, and Bulgarians. The German Austrians saw a threat to their well-being in these peoples.

The Slavic peoples had inhabited great stretches of central and eastern Europe for centuries. Austria itself had long been home for many of them. In truth, the German Austrians constituted only about 30 percent of the country's population. But they had always been a dominant minority. They controlled the nation's economic, cultural, and political life. Their domination can be most clearly seen in the fact that their language, German, was the official language of Austria.

The German Austrians had been able to exercise such power

because so many of the Slavs in their midst were peasants who remained close to the land and left the running of the country to others. It was a situation that, long ago, had led to one inevitable result. Great numbers of German Austrians had come to see the Slavs as their inferiors, a people of rude manners, little intelligence, and scant learning who must always "be kept in their place." But now . . .

But now, with Austria and Hungary joined, the German Austrians were dangerously outnumbered by their "inferiors." Further—and here was the real threat—the Slavic people weren't "keeping in their place" anymore. They were on the move in the new empire. They were demanding better jobs, an improved position in society, and a strong voice in the affairs of government. If something weren't done—and done soon—the German Austrians could see just one fate for themselves. All their powers of old would be snatched away. They would become the inferiors of the inferiors.

What could be done? To many German Austrians, there seemed but one answer. There must be what they called *Anschluss*. They must break their country away from Hungary and rejoin Germany. Their battle cry became *Deutschland uber Alles* (Germany over all). Their disdain of the Slavic peoples around them intensified into hate, the hate kilned of fright.

Such was the Austria into which Adolf Hitler was born. Such were the events that were to fire his interest in politics. And such were the bigotries—bigotries against all things non-German—that he was to make his own.

The fire was ignited when, at about age ten, Hitler came across two German magazines. Filled with pictures of battle, they were devoted to a war that Prussia had fought in 1870, just four years after defeating Austria. Declared by a France that wanted to stem the growing power of the German state, the Franco-Prussian war had lasted for just a few months.

Again, Prussia's magnificent army had proved unbeatable. France, an age-old German foe, had been thoroughly humiliated and was made to cede some of her lands to Prussia.

The two magazines captivated the boy with their stories of Prussian victories. He saw the Prussian soldier as the finest in the world, daring and fearless. He was prouder than ever of his German heritage. For a time, the neighborhood games of cowboys and Indians were put aside and replaced by pretend battles in which he always appeared as a Prussian officer. Then a disturbing question crossed his mind. Since Austria and Prussia were both German countries, why hadn't Austria joined in the fight against the hated French?

It was then he learned that Austria was no longer allied with Prussia but was now wedded to Hungary. With that, his political education began. In the next years, reading his books and listening to the adults around him, Hitler came to share their fears that Austria's German population would quickly be relegated to second-class citizenship. He was soon seeing the Slavs as dangerous inferiors. At the same time, his pride in being German intensified into a love of all that was German. By the time he departed for Vienna, Hitler was an ardent nationalist, one of the thousands of Austrians who wanted most in life to reunite with and become a part of Germany.

Even during the lost years in Vienna, the interest in politics never deserted Hitler. While first wandering the streets and while later sitting over his drawings in the Mannerheim, he went on reading about Austria's political affairs and her several political parties. He even took the time to make a study of the parties, a very practical study that was in sharp contrast to the aimless way he had chosen to live. Using the parties as examples, he set out to determine the factors that could make for political success.

He settled on four. First, he decided that the successful party must always use pageantry—from flag-emblazoned parades to massive rallies—to impress the people and draw them to its cause. Second, as its leader, you must never be content with the support of just the people. You must always seek the backing of the most influential and wealthy groups in the country. To your cause must be brought the major industries, the labor unions, the armed forces, the church. Without their money and influence, you could hope for nothing but failure. Without them, there was no real power.

Next, you must develop a massive and efficient propaganda machine to get your party's message to the people. That message must be repeated again and again. It must play on the fears and the wants and the hates of the people. It must hammer home the idea that you're the only one who can help them. There is no need to worry whether the message is the truth or a lie. Just repeat it often enough and loud enough. The people will soon accept it as gospel.

Finally, you must use what Hitler called a "spiritual and physical terror." As you gain power, you must make the people afraid to defy you and your party. In particular, your enemies must be cowed. If one causes trouble, you must unleash a "veritable barrage of lies and slanders" against him until he breaks down and runs. Terror, Hitler said, takes advantage of all human weaknesses. He believed that it could bring success with "almost mathematical certainty."

In fairness to Vienna's political parties, it must be said that historians do not believe that he developed the idea of terror from them. They were made up of decent and civilized men. It's thought that the idea emerged from his many readings and from his own mind.

The four techniques were cold-blooded ones. They did not originate with Hitler and, in truth, have been used throughout history by various ruthless leaders. In themselves, they are interesting ideas (in a terrible way), but it is even more interesting to note that, when he hit upon them, Hitler had no idea of entering politics himself. He was simply carrying out a study that had caught his fancy while he was still hoping for a life in art. But a sinister part of his mind seemed to be looking ahead to his real career. One day, the techniques would be put to work. Brutally.

Hitler's political thinking may have been cold and calculating. But not so another side of his thinking—his hatred for the Jews. It was hot and blind. And it would one day bear appalling political fruit.

4.

Hitler's anti-Semitism was shared by many Christian Europeans. In them, as in Hitler, it was a festering sore born of suspicion, ignorance, and superstition. For many, it was centered on the old accusation, now more than 1900 years old, that the Jews had crucified Christ. For others, it was centered in the anger and suspicion that can be so senselessly directed at anyone whose looks, dress, language, customs, and religious practices differ from those of the rest of the community. For still others, it was centered in an envy of Jewish enterprise and wealth.

In earlier centuries, the Jews had been barred by the Europeans from entering the crafts and professions. Though cut off from the principal occupations of the day, they had survived. They had started as moneylenders to the Europeans. (The European might dislike the Jew, but he was quite willing to borrow money from him when the need arose.) In time, they were servicing all levels of European society—kings who needed to finance a war, shopkeepers and factory owners who needed a business loan, the poor who needed money for tomorrow's food. From there, many Jews had gone on to prosper in banking, in business, in the arts, and industry. Theirs was a success that couldn't help but arouse an envy—so easily translated into hate—that reached out to touch all Jews, even the poorest of their number.

Added to the envy was the suspicion that many Jews had become the wealthiest people in Europe. There was even a rumor afoot that the wealthy Jew was out to control Europe by controlling its money.

Hitler learned of all these prejudices at some point in his early life and made them his own. Before he was done, he was to put them to insane use.

But at what point did he learn them? No one knows for certain. In *Mein Kampf*, Hitler speaks at length on how and why he became an anti-Semite. But here, as elsewhere in the book, his words are suspect. He may well be painting a picture that puts him in the best light possible and makes him seem a reasonable man rather than a blind bigot.

For whatever his word may be worth, Hitler claimed that his feelings for the Jews did not take shape until the Vienna years. He wrote that there was no reason for him to feel animosity as a child because there were so few Jews living around him. Also, Jews were never talked about in his home. He claimed that he could not remember the term "Jew" ever being heard "during my father's lifetime."

There were, he recalled, a few Jewish students at the Realschule. One "was treated by all of us with caution." But this was not because the boy was Jewish. It was simply that he was someone who could not be trusted. Further—an all-important point to a young German nationalist—Hitler said he thought the Jewish students to be no different from the other students. He "took them for Germans."

But then he came to Vienna. Here, in a city with a Jewish population of approximately 200,000, his feelings crystalized.

To hear him tell it in *Mein Kampf*, it all happened one day while he was walking along a street. He suddenly came upon "an apparition"—a man "in a black caftan and black sidelocks." Hitler stared. Then he studied "this foreign face, scrutinizing feature by feature." He had never seen a human being like this before. "Is this a Jew?" he asked himself. And then the ardent nationalist in him altered the question. It became: "Is this a German?"

In the light of Hitler's own dress during the lost Vienna years, his shock at the "apparition's" appearance is laughable. But there is nothing laughable about the next pages in *Mein Kampf*. Hitler wrote that he set out to answer his question. He began to read about the Jews (though he makes no mention of their titles, he very likely turned to many of the anti-Semitic books that were to be found in the city). He took to watching closely the Jews whom he encountered on the street. The more he saw of them, "the more sharply they became distinguished in my eyes from the rest of humanity."

He visited the Jewish districts of the city and once more the nationalist in him surfaced; he found that they "swarmed with the people which even outwardly had lost all resemblance to Germans." Worse, they were unclean. With heavy sarcasm, he wrote, "By their very exterior, you could tell that they were no lovers of water, and, to your distress, you often knew it with your eyes closed. Later I often grew sick to my stomach from the smell of these caftan wearers. Added to this, there was their unclean dress and their generally unheroic appearance."

Fine words from someone who himself wandered the streets in a stained overcoat, unbathed, with his hair unwashed and uncut. But there was more venom to come. In the next pages of *Mein Kampf*, Hitler accused the Jews of being behind the very worst that Austrian culture had to offer—the very worst newspapers, the very worst books, the very worst music, the very worst theatrical productions. The Jews were behind them all; they were responsible for a "spiritual pestilence worse than the Black Death of olden times."

Then came the accusation that they were responsible for much of the vice in the city. Hitler wrote that prostitution in Vienna was most easily seen in the Leopoldstat, a predominantly Jewish district. All you had to do, he advised, was walk through its streets and alleys at night to see the horror there.

On every count, in Hitler's view, the Jews were behind the spiritual and moral failures of all society. They were a menace to all Gentile Europeans, to all humanity. The man who claimed never to have heard the word "Jew" in his boyhood home was now their mortal enemy. He ended his tirade in *Mein Kampf* on a lofty note that, were it not for the atrocities of the future, would be comically pompous:

". . . today I believe that I am acting in accordance with the will of the Almighty Creator: by defending myself against the Jew, I am fighting for the work of the Lord."

Though Hitler claimed that his anti-Semitism took shape in Vienna, his boyhood friend, Gustl Kubizek, disagreed. Kubizek said that Hitler's prejudices were already well developed and neatly in place at the time they met in their teens. But it does not really matter when Hitler became an anti-Semite. What counts is that, by 1913, his hatred—and his passion for politics—had hardened into characteristics that would endure a lifetime. Both would one day leave the world irreparably scarred.

In that year, 1913, Hitler ended his Vienna stay. The twenty-four-year-old nationalist who loved everything German knew where he must now go. Packing his few belongings, he left the Mannerheim, crossed the border into Germany, and settled in the Bavarian city of Munich. There, within a few months, his life was suddenly to change. He was to go to war.

3. THE CRUCIBLE
OF WAR

卐

ONCE, WHEN RECALLING his stay in Munich, Hitler remarked that he had worked as a painter there. In later years, his political enemies used the statement to their advantage; they claimed that he had been a house painter and that the reins of government should not be placed in the hands of someone of such a lowly calling. There is, however, no evidence that Hitler ever painted a house in his life. By "painter," he obviously meant artist. His work: the drawing of a few commercial posters similar to those he had done while in Vienna.

Hitler remained in Munich through the rest of the 1913 and the first half of 1914. Then came the terrible upheaval that changed his life for once and all. War broke out in Europe.

Today, we know it as World War I, the first of the awful international conflicts that have scarred the twentieth century. But, in the four years that it raged—from mid-1914 to late

1918—and in the two decades that followed its close, it was known simply as the Great War.

The outbreak was triggered by the assassination of Archduke Francis Ferdinand of Austria by a secret society from the small country of Serbia, a nation that hated the Austro-Hungarian alliance. For years, a tangle of rivalries, treaties, envies, fears, and wants for each other's territories had threatened the nations of Europe with war. Now Ferdinand's death unleashed a storm of passions that had been kept bottled up for too long. There was a sudden and sickening choosing up of sides. Ferdinand died in late June, 1914. Little more than a month later, the Central Powers (Germany and Austria-Hungary) were squared off against the Allied Powers (France, Russia, and Great Britain, later to be joined by Italy and the United States). The stage was set for one of the great catastrophies of all time, a war that would claim 8 million lives.

The twenty-four-year-old Hitler, however, saw the war as anything but catastrophic. Rather, he saw only glory for his adopted country. Germany, with her splendid army, would quickly win through to victory, undoubtedly in a matter of weeks. She had been growing stronger and more unified through the years. Now, under her present monarch, Kaiser Wilhelm, she was sure to emerge from the fighting as the most powerful nation in Europe. His was a certainty shared by Germans everywhere.

And Hitler welcomed the war for more personal reasons. He had read history all his life. Now he was going to be a part of history, an *actual* part of it. So great was his joy at the terrible events in Europe that he later wrote in *Mein Kampf*: ". . . Even today I am not ashamed to say that, overpowered by stormy enthusiasm, I fell down on my knees and thanked Heaven from an overflowing heart for granting me the good fortune of being permitted to live at this time."

On August 3, 1914, Hitler volunteered for the army. Though Germany was now a unified country—a monarchy under Kaiser Wilhelm II—she was made up of independent states, each with its own government and each with its own military units that served alongside the national army and navy. Munich was located in the state of Bavaria and Hitler was assigned to the 2nd Bavarian Infantry Regiment. He spent a week of close-order drill, cross-country marches, and bayonet practice. Then he was transferred to the 16th Bavarian Reserve Infantry Regiment. He remained with the 16th for the entire war.

In October, 1914, with hardly ten weeks of service life behind him, Hitler went into combat. The German forces were pushing through Belgium on their way to France at the time and, in his first action, Hitler helped to capture a wooded area near the Belgian city of Ypres. He participated in the Belgian fighting throughout 1915. In 1916, as the Germans tried to beat their way deep into France, he served in the great battles along the Somme, Aisne, and Marne rivers. He returned to Belgium in 1917, but came south again in 1918, this time for the final big German push toward Paris. Finally, returned to Belgium once more, Hitler ended his war near Ypres, right where he had started. The end came in October of the year, when he was caught in a British gas attack.

The war quickly transformed Hitler from a wandering artist to a hardened soldier. An acquaintance who had trained with him was amazed at the change in Hitler when they met at the front a short time later. In training, Hitler had looked thin and frail, so frail that it didn't seem possible he could shoulder a full field pack. Now, at the front, the artist had become a rangy man who carried his rifle loosely and walked with an easy, confident gait, with his helmet set at a rakish angle. He was "the picture of the front line soldier," the friend said.

There is no doubt that Hitler was a good and dedicated soldier. Most of his service time was spent as a courier, running messages to companies in the trenches or out in "no man's land" from the regimental command post. It was an important job because telephone communications were often knocked out by enemy artillery fire. That he performed well can be seen in the regard that his fellow soldiers held for him. He had a reputation for being willing to take on the most dangerous deliveries. He was never suddenly "sick" in times of crisis. Nor did he ever complain of the filth, the vermin, and the mud of the trenches. His fellow messengers once watched in awe as he crawled, Indian-fashion, across a battlefield under heavy fire to deliver a communique. Those boyhood games of cowboys and Indians were now being played for real.

In later life, his political enemies were to accuse him of cowardice in the war. If his fellow soldiers are to be believed, the charges were groundless and politically motivated. The men may have disliked him on some other counts; his rabid interest in politics often got on their nerves and his habit of going off by himself to brood or to read prompted one soldier to say that "we have a white wolf"—an odd loner—"in our midst." But those who were interviewed in later years all admitted to an admiration for his fearlessness and his dedication to duty.

Even if his comrades had never spoken up, there is still ample evidence available of Hitler's daring. He was decorated several times for bravery. In 1914, with just a month or so at the front under his belt, he received the Iron Cross, 2nd Class. In 1917, the Military Cross, 3rd Class, came his way, followed in 1918 by the Service Medal, 3rd Class. His most distinguished award, which he also received in 1918, was the Iron Cross, 1st Class. One of the country's most prized medals, it rarely ever went to an enlisted man.

Hitler's first Iron Cross was earned on a November morning. With a fellow runner, he had ventured deep into a wooded area with his commanding officer to observe a stretch of enemy line. A British machine gunner sighted them. Suddenly, bullets began to spray the ground at their feet. Hitler and his fellow messenger grabbed the officer and shielded him with their bodies. Then they dragged him to the shelter of a ditch, after which they all crawled to safety.

The incident was a memorable one for Hitler. Even more memorable was the story behind his second Iron Cross almost four years later. It is possibly the most interesting story to come out of his army career. There is also an element of mystery surrounding it.

As the story goes, Hitler was working his way through a battle area one day when he sighted an enemy helmet showing just above the lip of a trench or a shell crater. He wormed his way forward on his stomach and then began to shout orders in German, sounding as if he had a full company with him. A group of enemy soldiers climbed out with their arms upraised in surrender. At gunpoint, Hitler escorted them back to regimental headquarters.

Where's the mystery? There is no written proof that the incident ever occurred. The story was passed down through the years by word of mouth, with Hitler's fellow soldiers telling it again and again. It became increasingly confused with the tellings. One friend said that the prisoners were French, another that they were British. One version set their number at fifteen. Another placed it at four.

Further, no mention was ever made of the feat in the regiment's official history. This was not, however, unusual. The history dealt with the accomplishments of the regiment as a unit and did not often mention those of individual soldiers. Quite as mysterious was the fact that there was no description of Hitler's action in the citation that accompanied his medal. The citation said only that the Iron Cross, 1st Class, was being awarded "for personal bravery and general merit." But there had to be something to the story. Remember, the medal rarely went to an enlisted man.

In addition to his reputation for courage, Hitler was also known as a lucky soldier. He had a number of close encounters with death and injury, only to escape unhurt. Miraculously, it often seemed.

His luck showed itself in his very first battle. As he was advancing on the wooded area near Ypres that morning, Hitler felt something pluck at his arm. When he took the time to look, he found that a bullet or a chunk of shrapnel had torn away the right sleeve of his coat. His arm was untouched.

On another occasion, he and three companions were seated in a tent that was serving as regimental headquarters. They were forced to leave so that there would be room for several officers who had just arrived for a meeting. No sooner had Hitler and his friends walked off than a British shell crashed into the tent. Hitler's commander was injured. The visiting officers were killed.

Years later, he told a British journalist of his most miraculous escape. He recalled that, while eating dinner in a trench with a group of soldiers, a voice came to him. In a tone so sharp and clear that it seemed to be giving a military order, the voice told him to move away. He stood up and carried his mess gear along the trench to a spot about twenty yards distant. Moments later, there was an explosion and a blinding flash. A stray enemy shell had dropped on the spot where he had been sitting. His dinner companions all died in an instant.

Hitler's luck was such that his friends thought he was blessed with a "charmed life." They liked to be near him. As one of them remarked, "If you're with Adi, you'll be safe."

But no combat soldier can be lucky forever. Hitler was wounded twice in the course of the war. Harm first came his way on the night of October 7, 1916.

On that night, Hitler had just settled down to sleep in a small tunnel leading to regimental headquarters, which was then located underground in a trench. With him were a number of other runners. They all tried to sleep in an upright position, with their backs pressed against the earthen walls. Suddenly, a shell burst in the mouth of the tunnel. The runners were sent sprawling in every direction. There were screams as metal fragments tore into them. When it was all over, a dazed Hitler found that he had been hit in the leg.

The wound—in fact and in his view—was not serious. Hitler told his commanding officer that he wanted to remain on duty. But he was carried off and sent to a hospital near Berlin. He remained there for eight weeks.

Far more serious was the harm done by the gas attack in October, 1918, almost exactly two years later. The attack came during a heavy British bombardment. Abruptly, along with the sound of the crashing explosions, the air was filled with a sickening odor. A mist spread over the ground. All around Hitler there were terrified shouts of "Mustard gas!" Quickly, clumsily, with hands trembling, the men pulled on their gas masks. Then they sat huddled together while the awful fumes swirled about them, burning them wherever their skin was exposed. The bombardment ended in the early hours of the next morning and the air was clear again by dawn. With sighs of relief mingling with groans of pain, the masks came off . . .

But too soon. The bombardment started again. Explosive shells and gas shells pounded down on the men. Once more, the air was filled with the sickening mist. It caught Hitler, burning into his eyes and face, before he could tug his gas mask into place. He felt his eyelids swell. Tears poured helplessly down his cheeks. His vision blurred. In seconds, he could see little or nothing. He was almost totally blind when helping hands finally led him away to safety.

Temporary blindness or near blindness is one of the classic results of mustard gas poisoning. Hitler was sent to a hospital at Pasewalk, a town in northern Germany. There, at first certain he would never see to read or paint again, he began a slow recovery. And there, just scant weeks later, on November 11, 1918, he heard that the war had ended in terrible defeat for his country.

2.

Hitler was an angry as well as a wounded soldier in that November. His anger was not directed against the British who had blinded him. Rather, it bore in on the German people themselves, civilians and servicemen alike. He felt that countless of their number had been guilty of cowardice over the years. It was they, and not the enemy, who had finally brought the nation to its knees.

For Hitler, their cowardice dated back to 1916. By late that year, the war that had begun so gloriously had become stalemated. There had been no great victories and no great advances by either side. Rather, the enemy forces had carved networks of trenches across the face of northern France and had settled down to a brutish fighting that led nowhere—fighting that saw one side or the other take a few yards or a few miles of ground on one day and then lose it all on another. It was fighting that took a terrible toll in lives. And fighting that started to break the backs of the civilian population at home.

Soon rumors reached the front that the people at home were growing sick of the war. They were stricken by the loss of loved ones. They wanted life to return to normal. And, thanks to a highly efficient British blockade that prevented the arrival of needed supplies from friendly powers overseas, they were short of food and clothing. There was hunger everywhere, just as there was in the trenches. Families were forced to kill cats, dogs, and rats for food. Bread had to be made from sawdust or, if you were lucky, from potato peelings. Austria was almost out of wheat.

The word of the civilian discouragement and the desire to end the war enraged the battle-hardened Hitler. Had the people forgotten the glory that could be Germany's? The new strength that would come with victory? The new prestige? Why couldn't they sacrifice a few comforts and endure an empty belly? These things were as nothing when compared to the sacrifice made by a fighting man when he gave up his blood or his life. The talk at home was worse than cowardly. It was treasonable.

His fury boiled over when he saw the discouragement spread among his comrades. More and more, they had to endure his political outbursts about the harvest that victory would reap. Once, he became so enraged at a soldier's complaints that he threw himself at the man. They ended up rolling in the mud and pommeling each other. In later years, Hitler's friends recollected that both men came out of the tussle bruised and bleeding but that "Adi" was the clear winner.

Of all the cowardice he thought he saw, Hitler hated most the brand practiced by what he called "the slackers back home." In his view, these were all the men who had stayed out of uniform; they were now safe behind the lines, working in comfortable and profitable jobs. Assuredly, some were not in the service because of legitimate health reasons, but Hitler was certain that most of the stay-at-homes thought it "a sign of wisdom" to enjoy snug and secure lives while others risked the dangers of battle. His twisted anti-Semitism came rushing to the forefront. As far as he was concerned, all Jews were slackers. In one of *Mein Kampf*'s angriest passages, he wrote of what he saw on a furlough to Berlin: "The offices were filled with Jews. Nearly every clerk was a Jew and nearly every Jew was a clerk."

Additionally, he was convinced that the country's wealthiest Jews were in control of Germany's war production. The Jews, then, were not only slackers who left the fighting to Germans. They were also profiteers who fattened themselves at home while German blood was spilled at the front.

That his accusations were groundless can be seen in one fact alone. More than 100,000 Jews served in the German army during the war, with 12,000 of them losing their lives. Further, one of Hitler's own officers was a Jew—the respected First Lieutenant Hugo Gutmann. Gutmann was the man who, in 1918, first recommended that Hitler be awarded the Iron Cross, 1st Class.

In 1917, however, Hitler had been able to forget his anger for a time. The German situation had brightened when a revolution broke out in enemy Russia because of widespread discontent over the way in which the Czar was conducting the war. People there were as war-weary as the Germans. The Czar was dethroned. A republican government was established. But it, too, fell and Russia went to the Bolsheviks, a revolutionary group that had long sought to replace the Russian monarchy with a Communist government. Once under the Bolsheviks, Russia dropped out of the war. A sigh of relief went through Germany. Since 1914, she had been forced to fight on both the Russian and French fronts. Now that the danger on the East had disappeared, she could concentrate all her energies on the West.

It was in March of 1918 that Germany set out to win the long-stalemated Western war. Under the command of General Erich von Ludendorff, a massive force erupted from the trenches in northern France and plunged toward Paris. It swept to within fifty miles of the city before being flung back by the Allies. Then the Allies—strengthened by newly arrived troops from the United States, which had entered the war in 1917—spent the summer literally smashing every German maneuver. The great campaign that was intended to bring a final victory for Germany ended in disaster. Her army was torn to shreds by autumn. Though she was to fight on for another few weeks, her doom was sealed.

Now, in October and November, there came what was to Hitler the greatest cowardice of all. Sick of the war and knowing it was irretrievably lost, thousands of Germans turned on the monarchy that had gotten them into the conflict.

Workers went on strike. Army and navy units mutinied. There were political uprisings everywhere, led by forces that wanted to see Kaiser Wilhelm II fall just as the Russian Czar had fallen—Communist and Socialist and democratic forces that had long opposed the monarchy and hoped to put in its place some kind of people's government. In all, the entire nation collapsed. The governments in a number of its states fell; they were immediately replaced by local opponents. Next door, disposing of her ruler, Austria became a republic. The chaos reached its peak when Kaiser Wilhelm II abdicated his throne and fled Germany. The leading political party in Berlin—the Social Democratic Party—took over from him and prepared to sign an armistice with the Allies.

By early November, Hitler's vision was slowly returning. From his hospital ward, he followed the news of the nation's collapse. He could hardly believe what he was hearing. His beloved Germany of old was disappearing. He was sure the Jews and Communists were behind the new governments that were taking over the various states (as indeed the Communists were in a number of instances). He hated the Communists quite as much as the Jews; the heart of communism lay in Russia and he reasoned that, if the Communists were allowed to take power in Germany, they would turn it into a Russian-dominated state. In time, in his twisted view, Jews and Communists came to mean the same thing. It was a view that he would use repeatedly for political advantage in future years.

Toward midevening on November 9, Hitler was talking with several fellow patients in a little hall at the hospital. Suddenly, a local minister burst into the room. He was weeping and he brought terrible news. For the first time, Hitler learned that the Kaiser had abdicated. For the first time, he heard the inevitable—that the country was going to give up and ask for an armistice, with a formal peace treaty then to be worked out.

The news shattered him. He couldn't sit still. He jumped up and paced the room. Then his vision, by now almost fully restored, deserted him. In his hysteria, he was blind again. As he wrote in *Mein Kampf,* ". . . everything went black before my eyes; I tottered and groped my way back to the dormitory, threw myself on my bunk, and dug my burning head into my blanket and pillow."

His world, as he himself did, lay in ruins. Germany had lost her bid for greatness. Millions of her finest young men were dead or hopelessly maimed. She was going to grovel before the hated Allies. All that the future held was humiliation.

A hot anger merged with his sorrow. He could not bring himself to believe that Germany had been honorably defeated on the battlefield; the army had suffered terrible setbacks, yes, but they were only temporary; the troops could regroup, attack again, and win through to a final victory. No, Germany hadn't lost on the battlefield. She'd lost because of all the cowardly ones back home—the complainers, the spineless ones who couldn't stand a little hunger, the slackers, the Jews, the Communists, the politicians who were now going to beg for an armistice. They'd all stabbed her in the back.

Hitler was not alone in this conviction. The "stab in the

back" theory was held in the next years by thousands of Germans who couldn't swallow the embarrassment of admitting that their splendid army had been beaten. They needed some scapegoats. In particular, they chose the Social Democratic Party because it had sued for peace in the wake of the Kaiser's abdication. They said that only the army should have requested the armistice but hadn't done so because it knew it could rise again. The Social Democrats, then, were at fault. They had sent Germany to her final humiliation. Its members were soon dubbed "the November criminals."

The hard truth of the matter was that, following the disastrous summer of 1918, the army's top generals told the Kaiser their troops had been bested once and for all and could not fight on much longer. But, fearful of the terrible loss of face it would bring, they made no public announcement of this fact. Then, when the Kaiser abdicated, the generals continued to hold their silence while the party took the blame for the armistice and the formal peace treaty that followed it in a few months. Their reputations were safe.

As that night of November 9 deepened, Hitler's sorrow and anger chilled themselves into a steel resolve. He knew that, at the start of the war, he had been no more than a dreamy-eyed boy. But he had survived the crucible of battle. He had become a man. A hardened man who somehow must help his adopted country back to the strength and greatness she deserved. He must forget all his old dreams, all his dreams of art. . . .

As he was to write in *Mein Kampf* years later, "That night I resolved that, if I recovered my sight, I would enter politics."

It was one of the most fateful decisions ever to be made in the twentieth century.

4. BIRTH OF A POLITICIAN

THE ARMISTICE WAS signed on November 11, 1918, and the army doctors released Hitler from the hospital three weeks later. With his vision again returning to normal—though he later claimed that he could read nothing more than newspaper headlines at the time—Hitler traveled south through Germany to rejoin his regiment, which was now back in Munich. As he traveled, by train and by truck, the half-blind soldier wondered how he would ever get started in politics. He recognized that he had little practical background for the work. He had no profession. No history of responsible jobs. No friends of influence. Not even a high school diploma.

He did not, as he later admitted in *Mein Kampf,* "possess the least basis for any future action." All that he had going for him was determination. And years of reading history. And, as had been demonstrated in his Vienna analysis of the techniques that made for political success, a cold and calculating mind.

Wherever he looked as he moved south, Hitler saw chaos. He saw starvation. He saw hordes of jobless soldiers—men were now being released from the army in droves—wandering aimlessly here and there. Some were forming themselves into outlaw brigades and were raiding the countryside for food or joining in the political uprisings that were still taking place everywhere. In Berlin, Friedrich Ebert of the Social Democrats, the party that had taken over from the Kaiser, was heading a temporary national government. Ebert was calling for the country to establish a permanent democratic government, but the Communists had surrounded Berlin and were trying to throw him out of office. Hitler had little use for democracy—he thought it too inefficient an instrument to get things done properly—but he was happy when the Reds were repulsed. He had even less use for them.

In Munich, the capital of the state of Bavaria, the situation was just as hectic. A Jewish writer named Kurt Eisner had taken over the government there a few weeks ago. In the near future, he would be assassinated. The Communists would grab control for a time. Then they, too, would fall. Eventually, Bavaria would become a democratic state in the new Germany.

Despite his resolve, Hitler took no part in the political events of the day upon his arrival in Munich and in the months that followed. At first, he was stationed in the city itself and then was assigned to guard duty close-by the Austrian border for a time. Only once did he come near the political scene. He helped to keep his barracks from joining the short-lived Communist grab for control. In *Mein Kampf*, he recalled that the local Red leaders wanted to arrest him for his work in the barracks. He avoided jail, he wrote, by snatching up his rifle and pointing it at the three men—"scoundrels," he called them—who came to take him in.

The future politician did, however, keep close tabs on the events sweeping Germany. In January, 1919, he saw Friedrich Ebert's efforts to establish a permanent government begin to bear fruit. Named in a national election that month were 423 delegates who were to meet and draw up a constitution for a new Germany. Then, in the next month, Hitler read of how they were gathering at the city of Weimar 150 miles south of Berlin. There, they drafted the constitution for what was soon being called the Weimar Republic.

Under the constitution, Germany became a democracy for the first time in its history—a federal republic. It was to consist of seventeen states, of which Hitler's Bavaria, with its capital still at Munich, was to be one. Each state was to maintain a government for running its own affairs. The national government and a national parliament were to be housed at Berlin; the citizens would elect their representatives in the parliament. The country was also to have an elected President. He was to appoint a Chancellor. The Chancellor, assisted by a cabinet of ministers, would function as the nation's chief administrative officer.

Then, in June of that year, Hitler read that Germany and the Allies had agreed on the terms for a formal peace treaty. The treaty, which was signed at the Palace of Versailles in France, was a harsh one. It forced Germany to admit that she had started the war. It demanded that she pay huge reparations, in cash and industrial goods, for the damages suffered by the Allied nations in the fighting. She was also to return all the lands west of the Rhine River that had been won from France in the Franco-Prussian war back in 1870; included in them were some of the richest industrial areas in Europe. Finally, she was to limit her army to a scant 100,000 men and was not again to build warships, tanks, airplanes, or any other weapons of war.

For Hitler and Germans everywhere, the agreement was not

only harsh but also humiliating. It left Germany on her knees, strapped with reparations totaling millions of marks. It threatened never to allow her to rise and become strong again. Hitler read its details in a cold fury. They gave him another weapon for the future. The day would come when he would use the treaty—along with his hatred of the Jews, the "November criminals," and the Communists—to bring millions of Germans into his political party.

Political party? When, he asked himself, would he ever be part of a political party? The war had been over for several months and he had yet to take one step toward entering politics. Insignificant soldier that he was, he wondered if he would ever be able to take that step.

Actually, his political career was about to begin.

2.

The German army—the Reichswehr—gave Hitler his start in politics.

The army was sworn to support and uphold the Weimar Republic. On the surface, it seemed to do so. But, beneath the surface, it was anything but loyal. At the core of the trouble was the elite and aristocratic officer corps. These men wanted nothing of the Republic. They wanted a return of the monarchy of old. They had been at their most powerful under the Kaiser and they had an arrogant lack of faith in the common man's ability to govern himself.

The army's dislike of the Weimar Republic was especially sharp in Bavaria. In fact, this most southern state in Germany was fast becoming a center of anti-Republic thinking. Aristocrats who, along with the officer corps, longed for the monarchy were settling here. So were ardent German nationalists who detested the heads of the newborn Republic for signing the humiliating peace treaty. And so were disgusted officers who had been discharged from the service. The most prominent of the officers to set up housekeeping in Munich was General Erich von Ludendorff, the leader of the mighty—and, in the end, fruitless—German offensive of 1918.

Sometime in 1919, the army in Munich inaugurated a series of instruction classes for the men in the ranks. They were called "classes in civic thinking," but they were really indoctrination courses in the army's political views. They were conducted by leading teachers in the area, among them Professor Karl von Mueller of the University of Munich.

Hitler was sent to von Mueller's course. He found the man's talks fascinating and hung on his every word. Then Hitler was named to be his regiment's *Bildungsoffizier*—education officer. It was this assignment that really started him on his way in politics. He got the job because of an incident in von Mueller's class that caught the professor's eye.

There are two versions of the incident. In *Mein Kampf,* Hitler recalled that, during a class discussion period, a fellow student made the mistake of saying a good word about the Jews. Hitler jumped to his feet and delivered one of his anti-Semitic harangues. Impressed, von Mueller passed the word of Hitler's performance to his superiors. They were so pleased that they gave him his new assignment.

Von Mueller remembered things differently. Years later, he wrote that, as he was leaving the classroom one day, he passed a circle of students in heated discussion. Talking furiously in their midst was a soldier with a small and pale face, a shock of unruly hair, a close-cropped mustache, and pale blue eyes; Mueller recalled that the eyes glowed fanatically. The encircling men seemed to be held spellbound. Von Mueller went immediately to Hitler's superiors and told them that they had a "natural-born orator" on their hands.

One way or the other, Hitler became the regimental education officer. His instructions were direct and simple. In a continuing series of lectures, he was to alert the soldiers to the political dangers of the day as the army saw them—anti-monarchy dangers that ran from communism to socialism to democracy.

Hitler loved the job. At last, in the barracks and squad rooms of the regiment, he had one captive audience after another. At last, after years of haranguing his fellow residents in the Mannerheim and his comrades in the trenches, he could be something more than just participant in a discussion; he could be the center of attention. Further, as he had long suspected, he discovered that he had a genuine talent for speaking in public. His voice was full and strong. It could reach every one of his listeners, even those in "the farthest corners" of any room.

Early on, his listeners noted that Hitler had his own distinct way of delivering a speech. He would start slowly and softly, speaking in a gutteral voice and seeming to be calm, thoughtful, and reasonable. Then he would quicken his pace. His voice would become steadily louder; excitement, anger, and passion would break through. At last, accentuating his points by smashing one fisted hand into the open palm of the other—or by bringing the fist continually downward in a striking action— he would let himself go completely, with his voice now a shout and his words coming in a torrent. His listeners could not help but be swept along on the flood tide of his emotions. It was, many soldiers later agreed, the most effective speaking style they had ever encountered.

Very soon, the education officer took a further step into politics. Because of the devotion he gave to his lectures, Hitler's superior officers singled him out as a particularly competent worker. They had an extra assignment for him. He was to do some "investigative work." To put it bluntly, he was to spy on a local political group.

At the time, Munich was not just a center of anti-Republic sentiment. It throbbed with political beliefs of all kinds. There were more than fifty political organizations in the city, committed to everything from democracy to communism. No matter a man's ideology, and no matter whether he was serious thinker or just plain crackpot, he could find a place for himself somewhere in their ranks. They were mostly small groups, boasting anywhere from half a dozen to several hundred members, and they were mostly pretty harmless. Their members seemed to do little but sit in Munich's various beer halls discussing how to improve the world. The fact is, most were hardly more than social clubs.

Innocent and harmless though they might be, the army still wanted to keep track of what they were doing and thinking. Among the newest of the groups was the *Deutsche Arbeiterpartei* (German Workers Party) or DAP, as it was known by its initials. It was dedicated to replacing the Weimar Republic with socialism—a type of government that the army found equally repugnant. Hitler was told to take a look at the party.

Knowing only that it was a socialist organization, Hitler walked into the DAP's public meeting of September 12, 1919, and sat down on a wooden chair. He had been excited at the prospect of spying on a new and perhaps dangerous party, but his excitement evaporated as soon as he took in his surroundings. The meeting was being held in the back room of a beer hall. The room was darkish, the paint on the walls peeling, and the air dank with the odor of beer and tobacco smoke. There were perhaps twenty-five men in the audience. They sat quietly at round tables, sipping at foaming mugs. Their clothing was rough. They all seemed to be workingmen. How harmless could things be, Hitler wondered.

Several youngish men, obviously the party officers, sat at the head table. From the talk around him, Hitler learned that one of the officers—a smallish, sickly looking fellow with the gnarled hands of a laborer—was Anton Drexler. A toolmaker in the Munich railroad yards, he was the founder of the party. Most of the men in the audience seemed to be friends and co-workers of his. They were here because he'd talked them into coming.

Drexler called the meeting to order. Within a few minutes, Hitler found himself listening to the guest speaker of the evening—a local economist talking on how to eliminate capitalism. Hitler tried to follow the man's words with some interest. But it was no use. The whole thing was as dry as dust. The daring army spy wanted nothing more than to leave, return to his barracks, and write out a brief report (about three sentences would do) saying that the world had nothing to fear from the German Workers Party. Drexler and his followers would soon die of boredom.

But, always the dutiful soldier, Hitler remained where he was. The speech ground to an end and Drexler called for questions and comments from the floor. Then, with the suddenness that so often marked its onslaught, a hot anger poured through Hitler. His eyes bulged as he listened to a worker who had risen at a nearby table. The man was saying that Bavaria should break away from Germany and join with Austria to form a new country. The idiot was actually saying *that!* Actually!

In the next instant, the nationalist in Hitler had him on his feet. His outrage filled the room. How dare someone preach such nonsense, he demanded. No, not nonsense. Treason! Germany must remain united. It was the only way for her to survive her present humiliation. The only way for her to return to greatness . . .

His words came in a torrent. Every face was turned in his direction. Up at the head table, Anton Drexler was at first awe-struck and then delighted. He later recalled how he leaned over to the man next to him and whispered, "Now there's a real big mouth. We could use him."

Hitler at last sat down. There was a burst of applause. He couldn't help but feel pleased with himself. He'd given these dolts something to think about.

He'd also galvanized Drexler into action. As soon as the meeting ended, Hitler started for the door, only to hear the pad of footsteps behind him. A hand caught his sleeve. He turned to see an excited Drexler. He heard the little man ask his name and congratulate him on his remarks. Then there was some drivel about hoping that Herr Hitler would attend the future DAP meetings. It was all too silly. He was a soldier and a proud nationalist. He had no wish to join a collection of cow-faced fools. He escaped as quickly as possible.

In the morning, Hitler wrote a brief report on the meeting, describing it as harmless. Then he found that he hadn't escaped at all. The mail brought a postcard from Drexler. It informed Hitler that he had been accepted as a member of the party. He was invited to attend the next meeting of the organization's central committee. As he later wrote, Hitler didn't know whether to "laugh or be angry" over the card. How could the man be so stupid as to enroll him as a member without even asking permission?

But the card didn't land in the wastebasket. Hitler knew an opportunity when he saw one. He wanted the chance to enter politics, didn't he? Well, despite the smallness and the lameness of the group, this might be just what he was waiting for. At the least, it was worth looking into.

And so, making it clear to Drexler that he was not yet a member, Hitler sat in on the committee session. It was held in another back room, this one in a seedy restaurant. It surpassed the public meeting as a masterpiece in boredom.

Including Drexler, there were five committeemen present. To Hitler, they looked a shabby lot. He couldn't detect a strong figure among them. They all seemed too timid. And their behavior proved him right. First, they poked their way through the minutes of the previous meeting. Next, they read a couple of letters from people who wanted to get the DAP started elsewhere in the country. Then they talked about the aims of the party. And then they talked—on and on and on—about possible guest speakers for future public meetings. Before all the business was done with, Hitler could hardly control his impatience. This wasn't political action. This was club work. At its worst! He should have nothing to do with this bunch. He'd be wasting his time.

But, despite his annoyance, Hitler could not put the little DAP out of his mind when he finally left the meeting. A part of him still saw it as an opportunity, even though he fully realized that he'd be throwing his lot in with a band of ineffectuals who had no idea of how to build a powerful organization. Actually, it was the very smallness of the party that appealed to him. He'd have no trouble in soon taking over its leadership. He could then shape it as he wished and lead it wherever he wished. He could make it strong—and make a career for himself as its leader.

In *Mein Kampf*, Hitler wrote that the question of joining the party was the "hardest" he had ever faced. He said that he "agonized" over it for two days. Then: ". . . I finally came to the conviction that I had to take this step . . . It was the most decisive resolve of my life. From here there could be no turning back."

He made it sound all very dramatic, as if he sensed then what destiny held in store for him and the party. Some historians feel that his dramatic tone was unjustified. They believe that he joined not because he could see destiny beckoning but simply because there were no other opportunities on the horizon for this ambitious man who had set his sights on a career in politics.

Further, John Toland, in his biography, *Adolf Hitler*, points out that the army helped Hitler to his decision. At the time, a group of high-ranking officers and wealthy Bavarian businessmen were meeting quietly to talk about the rebuilding of Germany's military might, which was forbidden by the peace treaty. They believed the buildup could be accomplished only if the nation's war-weary workers got strongly behind it. Hitler's report on the DAP was passed to them. They agreed that the little party might one day be of help in bringing workers to their cause.

General Erich von Ludendorff was a member of the group. He went to Hitler's commanding officer and requested that the young man join DAP and do what he could to make it grow. The request was passed on to Hitler. In time, the general who had headed the 1918 offensive would join the party and become its most prestigious early member.

And so the decision was made at the end of September, 1919, though perhaps not as dramatically as Hitler liked to recall in later times. But it was a fateful decision. The thirty-year-old-soldier, the failed artist and former vagrant, was at last in politics.

3.

The members of the central committee had no idea that Hitler planned to turn their party into an active and growing force when he joined them. As he had seen, they were basically timid men who were content to let it remain a discussion club. Now, stunned, they found a whirlwind in their midst. Hitler immediately demanded that twice as many public meetings as before be held. It was the only way to build the membership. There must be, in his words, "mass meetings."

Objections came from every side: the DAP had neither the money nor the manpower for such an ambitious undertaking; the party must grow slowly, patiently. Brushing the whining aside, Hitler set a date for the first meeting on his own and rented a small hall. Next, back at the barracks, he typed out a string of announcements for the meeting, later buying an old mimeograph machine to get the job done faster. Then he went out into the streets, tacked the announcements up everywhere, handed them to passersby, and left them on the tables in beer halls.

Now that he had found his true calling in life, Hitler seemed possessed of a boundless energy. His industry paid off. The first meeting, which was held in October, drew thirty people. A week or so later, the next meeting boasted an audience of seventy. By year's end, attendance had hit the 100 mark. His greatest early triumph came in February, 1920. He hired one of Munich's largest halls—it could seat 1,000 people—and ended up with double that number on his hands.

Hitler's speaking ability was much responsible for the swelling attendance. Though each meeting featured a guest speaker, Hitler always set aside twenty minutes or so for himself. The word of his compelling style quickly spread. More and more people wanted to hear him. And more and more of their number wanted to join the party after listening to him passionately describe how it would fight to stamp out communism, seek to make Germany great again, and work to give the laboring man a better life.

His audiences were made up principally of working people who felt they had always been forced to live in poverty while their labors made the nation's capitalists richer and richer. Though not really a socialist himself, Hitler proved to be an excellent spokesman for the basic aim of socialism—the creation of a state that controlled a nation's production and distributed its wealth equally among everyone. He could speak fervently because the poverty of his Vienna years had made him hate capitalism and what were to his mind its most detestable representatives—the wealthy Jews. But his feelings for socialism went no deeper.

Had his listeners been able to see into his mind, they would have found him already a two-faced politician. On the surface, he was advocating a better life for workers. But, underneath, he was beginning to visualize another kind of government. One that would help the workers, yes. But one that would give them no power and no right to govern themselves. One that would be led by a strong man who would make the nation great because he knew what was best for it and because his word was law. A dictatorship.

Despite the successful meetings, the central committeemen were as nervous as ever. Hitler, the whirlwind, was moving far too fast. And, though he was just a new member of the committee, he was behaving as if he were the head of the whole thing. But they weren't so nervous as not to appoint him the party's information chief in early 1920. They had to admit that, with his busy typewriter and mimeograph machine, he really knew how to spread the news of the DAP's activities.

It must be said that not all members of the committee were opposed to the party's rapid growth. One new committeeman backed Hitler's tactics wholeheartedly. He was a professional soldier named Ernst Roehm. The two men soon became close friends.

Roehm was a tough, brutish-looking man who, oddly enough, was blessed with a quick and charming smile. Stockily built

and somewhere in his thirties, he had a thick neck, a blunt
face, and small, glinting eyes. His face was badly scarred. A
bullet had torn away the upper part of his nose in the war.
With Hitler, he hated the "November criminals" and wanted
to see Germany great again. He sensed in Hitler the makings
of a strong and determined leader.

At the time they first met, Roehm held the rank of captain
and was stationed at army headquarters in Munich. He watched
the swelling attendance at the meetings and realized that trouble
with the other political groups in the city lay ahead. Growing
as it was in popularity, the DAP was sure to arouse the anger
and envy of its rivals. Roehm guessed that there would soon
be attempts to break up the meetings. He was right. Hecklers
began to appear. More and more, there were derisive shouts
when Hitler tried to speak. Punctuating the shouts were flying
beer mugs.

The DAP had by now attracted a great many ex-soldiers
to its ranks. Roehm called the toughest of their number together. Dressing them in brown shirts, heavily buckled belts,
and black boots, he welded them into a small, rugged force
that could quickly put down any move against Hitler.

His men—many of them hardened street thugs—worked well
right from the start. With not a weapon in sight, they would
station themselves around the walls of the meeting room. They
would stand quietly by until the first sign of trouble. Then
they would move with lightning quickness. Out would come
truncheons and riding crops. The troublemakers would be
beaten to the floor and then hustled outside—if possible, all
in a matter of seconds.

Roehm's band of toughs quickly became Hitler's private
army. He gave it the name *Sturmabteilung* (Storm Detachment).
Soon known throughout Munich as the Storm Troopers, the
Brown Shirts, or the SA—its initials—it not only protected

Hitler from abuse but took to breaking up the meetings of rival parties. At first, it numbered about 200 men. Over the coming fifteen years, as Hitler's power spread across Germany, it was to grow to a force of more than 300,000.

In late March, 1920, Hitler left the army. Now, freed of daily military duties, all his energies went into the party. He rented a small office for his headquarters and equipped it with a desk, a telephone, and his faithful typewriter and mimeograph machine. He planned bigger meetings. He wrote pamphlets and outlined the aims of the DAP. He even managed to scrape up enough money to buy a small and bankrupt newspaper, the violently anti-Semitic *Volkisher Beobachter*. It became the party's official newspaper.

In the midst of all this activity, there was time for even more work. Hitler decided that the DAP must have a flag, one that would compete for the workers' attention with the now famous red banner of communism. Dozens of suggestions for the flag's design came from friends and party members. Hitler studied them all and spent hours trying to work them into a compelling final design. At last, he settled on a suggestion from a dentist. He would use the swastika.

Known as the "twisted" or "broken" cross, the swastika was an ancient symbol that had been known in many parts of the world. It had even been found among the Indians of North America. The word itself came from the Sanskrit and meant "all for all." Symbolically, with its bent arms, the cross represented the wheel of the sun or the cycle of life.

The flag that Hitler finally developed consisted of a solid red field with a large white disc at its center. Within the disc was emblazoned the swastika. Hitler arrived at its final design slowly and each part of the flag had great meaning to him. He said that the red field symbolized the socialistic ideas behind the party. The white disc symbolized his nationalist hopes for

Germany. The swastika represented his mission to struggle for the country's victory over the inferior peoples surrounding it.

In addition, Hitler designed a standard from which to drape the flag during meetings and parades. The design came from the standards carried by the ancient Roman legions. There was, first, a long vertical pole and then a horizontal black crossbar at its top. Attached to the center of the crossbar was a black metal swastika surrounded by a silver wreath. An eagle was perched above the wreath. Below the wreath was a metal triangle with the party initials printed on it. The flag, with fancy cords flowing down alongside it, hung from the crossbar.

From the moment of their design, the flag and its standard were seen—in the dozens and then the hundreds—at all party meetings and parades. Here, Hitler was putting to work one of the techniques for political success that he had developed back in Vienna. People were impressed by and attracted to pageantry. He was beginning to give it to them.

Hitler's various activities delighted the group of military officers and Munich businessmen who were secretly talking about rebuilding Germany's armed might. Quickly and efficiently, he was shaping a party of workers that they could bring to the support of the buildup. Hitler learned of their pleasure with his work and took full advantage of it. He began to cultivate their friendship, especially that of General Ludendorff. He had them introduce him to other wealthy Bavarians. And he asked them for—and received—some financial support for the DAP. They might have plans for the party, but he also had plans for them. He would use them and their kind more and more as time went on.

Another of his techniques for political success was being set in motion. A political party, even though it was dedicated to the poor worker, had to have the support of the rich and powerful if it was to have a hope of surviving.

Though he was becoming a friend of the rich, Hitler lived in near poverty during the years following his army release. His dedication to the building of the party can be seen in his way of life. He took no salary for his work, with all the funds received from member dues and elsewhere being used for DAP activities. Consequently, he could afford nothing more than a bedroom apartment that was hardly larger and hardly better furnished than his cubicle back at the Mannerheim. His clothes were as cheap and threadbare as the apartment. Whatever little money he had for himself came from speaking engagements for friendly or interested groups outside the party. DAP members often helped out by having him to their homes for meals. Some of the party's wealthy supporters slipped him a little spending money now and again.

For the three years between September, 1919, and late 1923, Hitler lived a zealot's hand-to-mouth existence, thinking only of the party. By 1923, because of his efforts, the DAP had grown from a collection of timid men around a back-room table to an organization boasting 35,000 members; though not yet well known elsewhere in Germany, it had become a power in Bavarian politics, such a power, indeed, that it was able to attract 100,000 people to an outdoor rally held with three similarly minded groups. And, by 1923, Hitler had replaced Anton Drexler and had become the party's undisputed leader. With his dominating personality and with the support of Ernst Roehm's SA, now 5,000 strong, no central committeeman dared to challenge any of his ideas and plans.

Finally, by 1923, the party had changed its name. Hitler called for a name that would assist the party in entering national politics and that would draw a greater number of workers to it. The result: he was soon at the head of the National Socialist German Workers Party (*Nationalsozialistische Deutsche Arbeiterpar-*

tei). Its initials were NSDAP. It was soon simply known as the Nazi Party.

Hitler's future in politics looked bright in that year of 1923. He was now so strong locally that he felt the time had arrived for his next step. He must now advance to the national scene. But then came November . . .

And disaster.

5. THE NOVEMBER ADVENTURE

HITLER, NO MATTER how great his energies, did not build his NSDAP through his own efforts alone. He was helped greatly by the political and economic problems besetting Germany. They were as bad as they had been at the end of the war.

For one thing, the infant Weimar Republic was in trouble. It was constantly being criticized and attacked from the outside by all the forces—from monarchist to Communist—that wanted to see it overthrown. From within, the members of its parliament kept it from ever becoming a strong government. A number of rival parties were represented in the parliament, with not one of them being in the majority. They feuded among themselves continually, knocking down each other's proposed legislation, with the result that Germany was never given a definite program for solving her many ills.

Then there was the specter of inflation—the decline in value of a nation's currency so that a consumer is able to buy less and less with his earnings. It had been around since the end of the war and was caused in great part by the fact that the Weimar government printed great amounts of paper money to help the country pay its war reparations and other debts. There was not enough gold and silver in the national treasury to back up the new money. As a consequence, the value of the German mark fell steadily through the years from 1918 to 1923.

In 1923, the problem got out of hand, suddenly and tragically. The mark went into a terrible slide and runaway inflation swept the country. At the start of the year, the mark had been valued at about four to one United States dollar. It dropped to 18,000 to the dollar in January. It continued to plunge until it was down to 160,000 to the dollar in July. By August, it reached the impossible low of 1 million to the dollar. It was in the trillions to a dollar by year's end.

The German economy lay in ruins. Families saw the savings of a lifetime wiped out. Sacks of money were needed to buy the merest of groceries. At one point, 2 million marks had to be carted to a bakery by anyone who needed to buy a loaf of bread.

The awful plunge did not take place without reason. Behind it were the French. In 1922, Germany fell so far behind in her reparations payments that she asked the Allied nations for permission to discontinue them for a time. All the nations agreed—except France. French President Raymond Poincaré said that his country had suffered greatly in the war and must be paid—one way or the other. And so, in January, 1923, he dispatched troops to take over the Ruhr district, German's chief industrial area.

The troops marched over the border and ran into a hornet's

nest. Infuriated, the German workers refused to cooperate with them. There were strikes. There was sabotage against the intruders. In a matter of days, there was guerrilla warfare. All industry in the Ruhr ground to a halt. At that point, with the nation's industrial underpinnings knocked away, the inflation of the past years went out of control.

Germany's myriad problems played right into Hitler's hands. The NSDAP leader raged against the Weimar Republic for not giving the country strong leadership. He raged against the printing of paper money that had fed the inflation. He raged against the runaway inflation. He raged against the Ruhr takeover. He raged, and a swiftly growing number of Bavarians, all of them terrified at what the future held, listened and saw in him a tough leader who could make things right again.

By early 1923, Hitler knew that the time had come for his move to the national scene. Launched was a campaign to catch the eye of the whole country. Hitler staged larger and larger meetings, parades, and rallies; in one parade, 5,000 smartly dressed SA troopers marched past as he stood on the reviewing stand and took their salute. He let it be known that he was the friend of such powerful figures as General Ludendorff; he made certain that he stood alongside the General on the speaker's platform during one giant rally. He urged the development of the Nazi Party throughout Germany.

But he ran into trouble in September. The struggling Weimar Republic began to solve Germany's economic problems. Arrangements were made with the Allied nations for Germany to continue her reparations payments at a much reduced rate. Further, there was a huge Allied loan in the works, one that would help the country get back on her feet. And the French were tired of the resistance in the Ruhr and were thinking about pulling out. Once they were gone, Germany's industry could begin to roll again.

All this was the worst of news to Hitler. He was thriving on the chaos. But it seemed about to end. After all the years of postwar struggle, Germany seemed about to move toward economic stability. If so, the fear would go out of the people and Hitler's chances of winning a national audience would plummet.

There was no time to waste. Something had to be done to make him an immediate national figure.

But what?

Secret meetings were held throughout September and October to hit upon a plan. They were attended by Hitler's closest friends and advisors, amongst them Ernst Roehm and two men fairly new to the party. The newcomers were Rudolf Hess and Hermann Goering.

Other than a liking for Hitler, a violent anti-Semitism, and an interest in aviation, the two men had little in common. Hess was a brooding man, tall and slender, dark-skinned, bushy-browed. The son of a well-to-do trader, he had been raised in Egypt. He served as an infantryman and then as a flyer in the war, after which he studied economics at the University of Munich. He joined the party upon hearing Hitler speak just once. His anti-Semitism caught Hitler's eye and he was soon brought up to the central committee. In time, he would become Hitler's personal secretary and the deputy leader of the Nazis.

As for Goering, he was blondish and fair-skinned, an extrovert, a heavyset man who would one day be obese. His father had been a much-traveled diplomat and Goering had spent most of his childhood in military boarding schools. At the outbreak of the war, he joined the German air corps. That he was a splendid flyer there can be no doubt; he downed more than twenty enemy planes. With the signing of the armistice, he went to Sweden as a commercial pilot and, while there, met and married a young noblewoman, Carin von Kantzow. They soon moved to Munich, where Carin's wealth enabled them to live in a luxurious apartment while Goering studied economics. Hitler's anti-Semitism attracted Goering to the NSDAP and he began a career that would see him become Germany's highest-ranking military officer.

Out of the September and October meetings came a daring—and totally outrageous—plan. It called for Hitler and his Nazi Party to grab control of the Bavarian government by force. As head of a German state, Hitler would be thrust upon the national scene. There was even talk that the takeover would trigger a national revolution that would see him overthrow the Republic.

The plot was hatched because the three top leaders of the Bavarian government had enraged the nationalist in Hitler. They were as opposed to the Weimar Republic as he. But they were talking openly of getting out from under the Republic by seceding Bavaria from Germany and linking her with Austria. Hitler hadn't ever been able to tolerate that kind of nonsense, and he could stomach it even less now, coming as it did from three heads of state. But it gave him just the opportunity he needed. He could burst upon the national scene as the hero who had saved Bavaria for Germany.

Known in the press as "the three vons," the targets of Hitler's wrath were Gustav von Kahr, the state commissioner of Bavaria; General Otto von Lossow, who commanded the army in Bavaria; and Colonel Hans von Seisser, the head of the state's police. They had long ruled with an iron hand, and now they must go. But they must go in a certain way, Hitler insisted.

Though he knew his takeover would be applauded by every Bavarian loyal to Germany, he wanted to cause as little upheaval as possible. There must be no full-scale revolt that brought the Nazi forces up against the better-equipped police and army.

Rather, "the three vons" must be quietly captured. Once in Hitler's hands, they would be made to issue orders on his behalf to the army and the police. The state would be his—without the risk of an open fight.

Again, an old Vienna technique was being put to use. For political success, get the strong and the powerful—in this case, the local army and police—on your side.

The question of how to capture the three leaders presented the conspirators with a headache. The problem was that the three were rarely ever in the same place at the same time. Various plans for capturing them individually were discussed and discarded as too complex. Then the newspapers announced that Kahr, Lossow, and Seisser were to attend a public meeting of local business organizations. It was to be held on the evening of November 8 at the Buergerbraukeller, a large beer hall in the southern area of Munich. Hitler and his fellow conspirators nodded in agreement. They had been given the perfect opportunity.

2.

On the morning of November 8, instructions went out to Storm Troopers throughout Munich. They were to assemble at designated points just after dark. Then 600 troopers were to board trucks and head for the public meeting. Another force, commanded by Ernst Roehm, was to drive to the War Ministry in central Munich and take it over from the skeleton nighttime staff. The Nazis would then be in control there when General von Lossow was captured. They would make certain that his Hitler-directed orders to the army were obeyed to the letter.

As for Hitler, he and his circle of friends gathered at Nazi headquarters just after 7:30 P.M. They climbed into two cars and, with Hitler riding up front in the party's red Mercedes, drove to the Buergerbraukeller. On arrival, Hitler saw that the place must be crowded to capacity because an overflow crowd was jamming the sidewalks. He also saw his SA troopers pull up. They jumped down from their trucks and he stood quietly by while they quickly surrounded the building. Then, with his friends at his heels, he pushed his way to the front door where several policemen were holding the crowd back. He demanded to be allowed to enter even if there was no room inside. The guards, knowing they were up against a local celebrity, stepped aside.

Hitler strode across the foyer and looked into the hall. More than 3,000 people were there, all of them packed around tables and all of them drinking beer from stone mugs. Up on the stage, Kahr was addressing the audience. Behind him sat General Lossow and Colonel Seisser. Perfect. The mice were in the trap.

Hitler was wearing a trench coat. He pulled it off and his friends saw that he had dressed himself in formal attire—striped trousers, black tailcoat, and wing collar—for this most critical night in his career. One friend thought he looked more like a minor diplomat than a revolutionary about to overthrow a government. Then there was no more time for thinking. A detachment of Storm Troopers trotted in; several of their number set up a machine gun in the entrance to the hall while the rest formed themselves into a bodyguard unit behind Hitler. With his face a hard mask, Hitler pushed forward, followed by his entourage. Up on the stage, Kahr was in the middle of his speech.

Once inside the hall, Hitler began to shout for silence. The people at nearby tables swung about in surprise. But most of the audience was unaware of his presence and failed to hear his words. Perspiration broke out on his face. He climbed up on a table. A pistol appeared from beneath his black coat. He raised an arm and fired a shot at the ceiling. The explosion echoed round the room—and he got the attention he wanted.

In the shocked silence, Hitler, his arm still upraised, shouted that a "national revolution" had broken out. He was taking control of the Bavarian government. It would be unwise to resist him. His Storm Troopers had surrounded the building. No one was to leave. Everyone was to remain quiet. Otherwise, the machine gun in the entrance . . .

Despite his orders, pandemonium broke out. Here and there, people dove beneath tables to protect themselves. Angry shouts came at him from all sides. He saw, though, that no one was insane enough to bolt for the door and challenge that machine gun. He jumped down from the table and pushed his way through the jostling crowd to the stage. His hair was now damp with perspiration and plastered against his forehead; his wing collar was wilting. He still held the pistol upraised above the heads swirling all about him.

At last, he reached the stage and climbed the stairs to it. An army officer assigned to the job of protecting the three government leaders suddenly blocked his way. Hitler saw the man's hand go to his jacket pocket. In a swift move, Hitler brought his pistol against the officer's forehead. Kahr, still standing at the front of the stage, called for the officer to move away. Kahr was deathly pale. He fell back a step as Hitler approached.

Hitler took Kahr's place. He announced again that the revolution had broken out. All along, he had known the audience would be made up mostly of government supporters and so he wasn't surprised at the angry shouts and jeers that came back at him: How dare he try to overthrow an established government? Did he know how silly he looked in that funeral director's suit? Ignoring the insults, he promised that the trouble would be over in just ten minutes—just as soon as he had a few words with Kahr, Lossow, and Seisser. With that, he whirled on the three men and, at gun point, herded them to a small room offstage.

But the prediction of a new government in ten minutes didn't come true. Once in the offstage room, Hitler found himself up against three obstinate men. Despite his assurances that he meant them no physical harm, they refused to cooperate and surrender Bavaria to him, with Kahr saying flatly, "You can kill me if you wish." Then they went on to scoff that Hitler, regardless of his SA, didn't have the muscle to go up against the army and the police. He should quit and go home. Right now.

Hitler answered that, at this moment, Ernst Roehm was taking over the War Ministry. Then he said that the revolt had the full support of General Ludendorff. It was a claim that shook the trio. Though retired for several years now, Ludendorff was still remembered and admired throughout the army. He could swing many a unit over to Hitler's side. Hitler said that Ludendorff would arrive in a little while to speak on his behalf.

Here, Hitler was guilty of a half-truth. It was true that he had sent for Ludendorff earlier in the evening and that the General should be en route to the hall at this moment. But the revolt did not have the old soldier's support. It didn't have his support for the very simple reason that Hitler hadn't told him of the planned uprising. Hitler had been afraid that Ludendorff would object to all the dangers involved. Now he could only hope that the General, who had become so loyal to the party, would go along with things once he saw how far the situation had developed.

The wait for Ludendorff turned out to be a long one. Nervous and sweating, Hitler couldn't bear to remain confined in the small room. Leaving his three prisoners under SA guard, he hurried out to the hall. The crowd was still raging. Goering was up on the stage, trying—and failing—to restore order. Hitler stepped in front of him and pointed to the balcony. Unless order was restored, he shouted, he would have a machine gun placed there. That brought a moment of startled quiet. In that moment, Hitler launched into a speech that some listeners, for years afterward, called the mightiest of his career.

He started with the bluff that the "three vons" were ready to cooperate with him. Without any bloodshed whatsoever, a new government was taking power in Bavaria and he was now calling for a nationwide revolution to overthrow the useless Republic. He then went on to speak of what his Nazi Party would do for Bavaria, for Germany, and for all the German people. Some listeners estimated that he spoke for about thirty minutes, sweating, shouting, and steadily rising to greater heights of emotion as he went along—and completely extinguishing all the torrid opposition in the hall. The 3,000 people who had greeted him with such anger no longer saw him as a ridiculous figure in a flapping tailcoat. They were swept into a frenzy of support. They all ended standing—some of them up on tables—and cheering his every statement. He had used the threat of a machine gun to get their attention. Then his power as a speaker had done the rest.

Ludendorff arrived during the speech. Hitler left the thundering hall and joined the General in the side room. As Hitler had expected, Ludendorff was furious that the revolt had been staged without his knowledge and approval. But he'd taken a look at the Storm Troopers outside; he'd seen the wild enthusiasm of the crowd; and he'd learned that Roehm's detachment was now safely entrenched in the War Ministry. And so, as Hitler had also expected, the old man realized that it was too late to turn back. Grimly, he nodded his support.

To Hitler, events now seemed to move with lightning speed.

He heard Ludendorff advise the three prisoners to cooperate and he saw them bow, with varying degrees of reluctance, to the General. Delighted, he rushed onstage to tell the people of this latest development and to say that they were now free to return to their homes. Offstage again, he heard splendid news from the outside. Word of the revolt was spreading throughout Munich and there appeared to be a snowballing support for it. Led by the Nazis in their midst, some army troops were already coming over to his side, as were a number of police units. More than 1,000 student officers from the nearby Infantry School were marching on the hall to throw their lot in with him; even now he could hear the brass band that was accompanying them. SA troopers and party members were moving to take over telephone and telegraph offices, army posts, police stations, banks. Hitler was almost dizzy with excitement. The night was turning into a complete triumph.

There was, it seemed, only one trouble spot. Some SA troopers had run into an uncooperative battalion of army engineers. With his excitement now making it impossible for him to stand still, Hitler decided that he must personally do something about the problem. Again leaving the three prisoners under guard—this time in Ludendorff's care—he dashed off.

It was a fatal mistake.

He was gone just a short while. On returning, he found that Ludendorff had released the prisoners; they had said they needed to get to their offices so that they could issue the orders that would place the government, the army, and the police completely under Nazi command. Hitler nodded and approved the General's action. Only hours later, after he had returned to his own headquarters, did he learn the sickening truth of the matter. The "three vons" had never intended to cooperate with him and had tricked Ludendorff. They hadn't gone to their offices at all. Rather, they had escaped the city and, from a secret post, had issued orders that all official groups in the state were to oppose the uprising.

They were orders that were now being followed. No longer were the army and the police coming over to Hitler's cause. Those units that had first sided with him had been whipped back into line. Troopers and party members were being arrested. The army had surrounded Roehm's men at the War Ministry and had them under siege.

Hitler slumped into a chair. His face was suddenly old, lined with exhaustion and defeat. One misstep had done it. One misstep had brought his night of triumph crashing down around him in disaster. His revolt—his dream of a heroic entrance on the national scene—was, with wrenching suddenness, at an end.

For long minutes, a heavy black depression settled over Hitler; depressions such as this were to play an increasingly frequent role in his life as the years went by. He couldn't think. He didn't seem to have the strength to move.

But the men around him—Hess, Goering, and even Ludendorff—said that he must move. He must not sit timidly by and swallow defeat. Unless he now acted boldly, he'd be finished in politics, even the most humble of local politics. He'd be a laughingstock. Worse, he'd likely face years in prison—perhaps even execution—for treason. He must throw his SA against the army and the police and try to take the government by brute force. There was a weak shake of the head in reply. His troopers were tough street fighters, yes, but they were no match for the well-armed police and army. Further, the men on both sides were all good Germans—not filthy Communists and Jews—and he recoiled from the thought of them spilling each other's blood. He wanted to act. But what could be done that wouldn't end in bloodshed?

It was Ludendorff who came up with a solution. As much

as Hitler, he said, he wished to avoid a bloodbath. He proposed that he himself lead a contingent of Nazis in a march to rescue Roehm's men at the War Ministry. Because the building was encircled by army troops, Ludendorff was certain that his rank and reputation would keep everyone from firing on him and his followers. He would simply march through the guns, enter the Ministry, and join Roehm. Once inside, he would use all his prestige to bring the army over to the Nazi cause.

The plan was a daring and risky one. There were all sorts of *ifs* in it. What *if* Ludendorff were wrong about being safe from gunfire? What *if* some soldier lost his head for even a second, just long enough to pull a trigger? What *if* Ludendorff couldn't convince the army to join him once he was inside the building?

There was only one point that didn't have an *if* attached to it. Even if the plan failed, Hitler knew that his reputation would be saved. He wouldn't be a laughingstock. He would be a man who, in the face of defeat, had courageously tried to rescue a band of trapped followers.

Hitler stood up. It was now close to four in the morning. He told Goering to summon the Storm Troopers. They were to meet before noon at the Buergerbraukeller. The scene of last night's triumph would be the point of departure for today's desperate march.

3.

By 11:00 A.M. on November 9, some 2,000 Storm Troopers and a swirl of party members were assembled in the outdoor beer garden surrounding the Buergerbraukeller. Long minutes were spent shaping the men into a line of march. Sometime between 11:30 and 12:00 noon, they moved out toward the War Ministry.

Heading the parade was a small open van; flying eight red

Nazi banners, it was crowded with Troopers known for their marksmanship. Directly behind the van walked Ludendorff and a young officer who was his personal aide. Hitler, Goering, Hess, and other major party figures marched on either side of the General and just to his rear. Alongside Hitler was a longtime friend and ally, Max Scheubner-Richter.

Next in line came the Storm Troopers. Some marched in columns. Some rode in open trucks, with the barrels of their rifles and machine pistols gleaming dully above the wooden side panels. The last men in line were all the party members who had gotten wind of the march and had arrived to lend a hand. They wore anything from business suits to working clothes to uniforms from the war. Nazi armbands were to be seen everywhere.

The day was raw and overcast, with the strong feel of snow in the air. The marchers walked swiftly and steadily. They made their way past one police barricade without incident. Then they were entering the narrow street that led to the front steps of the War Ministry. Here, they came to a stop. And here, Hitler felt his stomach turn over. Up ahead was a barricade. But it was not manned by soldiers as had been expected. Rather, there were only state police standing in front of it. Suddenly, the old General seemed very vulnerable.

Hitler and his group moved past the van and stood facing the barricade. Without waiting for any sort of instructions, a man named Ulrich Graf—he usually served as Hitler's personal bodyguard—broke away from the group. He stepped forward and shouted for the police to move aside, pleading, "Don't shoot. His Excellency Ludendorff is coming!" Hitler himself then called for the police to surrender. At his side, to begin forming a cordon across the width of the street, Max Scheubner-Richter linked his arm through Hitler's. Hitler could see a growing confusion among the men at the barricade. He knew that many of them were Nazi sympathizers. But they dared not move aside. They were on duty. They had their jobs to consider.

The two forces stood staring at each other for a trembling moment. Then . . .

There was the jolting and deafening sound of a gunshot. A split second later, the cold air was filled with the roar of gunfire from both ends of the street. At Hitler's side, Scheubner-Richter screamed and fell; he was dead when he hit the pavement; with their arms linked, Hitler went down with him. On his other side, Hitler saw Goering drop and clutch wildly at his leg. Behind him, the Nazis were throwing themselves to the pavement or turning and running.

Only two men remained standing in the front ranks—Ludendorff and his aide. With the aristocratic bearing that only years of training and authority can bring, the old man strode toward the barricade. Without falling behind by even a step, his aide came with him. They passed silently between the police rifles. Not one hand dared to reach out and stop them. They slowly mounted the steps to the Ministry, two lonely and proud and futile figures.

The shooting lasted for no more than a minute, if indeed that long. In all the years that followed, no one could say for certain who had fired first. Each side blamed the other. But, in that awful moment, sixteen Nazis and three policemen died. When it had passed, the street was littered with moaning, wounded men. Goering was carried to a nearby store; there, his wound was dressed, after which he was driven away in a car. Hess simply disappeared; it was later learned that he had fled to Austria and Goering had gone to Sweden. Inside the Ministry, Ludendorff and his aide were arrested, as were Roehm and his Storm Troopers.

As for Hitler, he pulled himself slowly to his feet. Dazed, he could do little more than stare blankly at the horror all around him. He became aware of a searing pain in his shoulder and was sure that he had been wounded and then was puzzled when he could see no blood; it was later learned that his shoulder had been dislocated when Scheubner-Richter pulled him down. Suddenly, hands caught him and led him to a car. It sped away, left Munich behind, and took him to the country home of a wealthy friend.

He was to remain there for two days, trying to rest but thinking only of his failed revolution and of the death that had been all around him. Then the Bavarian police arrived and placed him under arrest for treason.

4.

Hitler and General von Ludendorff, in company with eight lesser ringleaders, were brought to trial in February, 1924, for what had now become known as the "Beer Hall Putsch" (uprising), so-called because it had been centered in the Buergerbraukeller. With them was Rudolf Hess, who had loyally returned from his Austrian hideaway to stand beside Hitler. Missing was Hermann Goering. He and his wife were still in Sweden.

The trial lasted for about a month. In the end, Ludendorff was acquitted, in great part because of his advanced age and his past services to the country; he returned to his home outside Munich and disappeared from Hitler's life. The lesser NSDAP ringleaders received sentences of varying lengths. Hitler himself was sentenced to five years imprisonment.

When compared to what he could have received, the sentence was a fairly light one and reflected the court's understanding of his widespread popularity in Bavaria. Treason usually called for life imprisonment. Further, he was an alien and could have been deported back to Austria. As soon as the sentence was imposed, his influential friends began working behind the scenes for his release. That they were successful is seen in the fact that he entered prison on April 1, 1924, and was released on December 20 that same year—less than nine months later.

Hitler and his fellow conspirators served their terms at Landsberg, a one-time fortress on a cliff above the Lech River to the west of Munich. His stay there was anything but unpleasant. To begin, there were his "un-prison-like" accommodations. He was assigned to the section reserved for political prisoners and was given cell 7—the same one that had housed him during the trial. It wasn't really a cell but a medium-sized bedroom, larger than his Munich apartment. Entered via an ordinary door, it was furnished with a bed, nightstand, writing table, chairs, and bookcases. Its windows, though barred, overlooked a lovely scene—the fortress gardens and the surrounding forest.

Further, Hitler was not required to wear a prison uniform. Photographs taken at the time show him in shirt, tie, and jacket. And he seemed to have been allowed an unlimited number of visitors. Party leaders, friends, and supporters were constantly calling on him and bringing him gifts. His favorite gift was a poppy-seed strudel, a pastry that was cooked for him weekly by a group of women admirers.

Then there was his daily routine. It was regimented but certainly not taxing and prisonlike. The mornings featured exercise periods in the outdoors. Breakfast and lunch were served in a common room, with Hitler seated at the head of the table and treated by his fellow prisoners more as a host than an inmate. He spent the afternoons in his cell and took his evening meals there. Afterwards, he lounged about the common room. He returned to his cell at 9:00 P.M. Lights were out for the night an hour later.

Soon after arriving at Landsberg, Hitler settled down to a task that had been on his mind ever since the putsch—the writing of a book on his experiences in politics. He wanted to call it *Four and a Half Years of Struggle Against Lies, Stupidity, and Cowardice.* His friends advised him against such a cumbersome title. Chosen in its place was *Mein Kampf,* meaning "*My Struggle.*"

Striding about his cell, Hitler dictated the book to the faithful Rudolf Hess. Though it was planned as the story of Hitler's rise as a Nazi, it ended up being a hodgepodge of many elements. There was talk in it of his early years. There were his political views. There were tirades against the Jews. And there were random thoughts on any topic that happened to cross his mind as he dictated—thoughts on marriage, music, the theater, opera, sex, literature, and even the comics in the daily newspapers.

Hitler did not manage to finish *Mein Kampf* before his release and had to complete the manuscript at the home of a friend in 1925. Later, he wrote a second volume. The first book was published in 1925. Later, the two volumes were put together and issued as a single book.

Mein Kampf was a badly written, rambling book in which Hitler tried always to present himself in the best and most dramatic light possible. The grammar was so poor that Hess and several friends had to work long hours correcting it. When first published, *Mein Kampf* sold fairly well among the party faithful. Then the sales plunged and remained pitifully low for the next years. But, when Hitler finally came to full power in Germany, the sales skyrocketed. Between 1933 and 1940, close to 6 million copies were sold.

Germans did not buy the book because they wanted to read it. Rather, they found it politically wise always to have a copy in view. Germans today recall that *Mein Kampf* was probably the most popular wedding gift during the late 1930s. Royalties from its sale eventually made Hitler a multimillionaire.

Historians agree that it's a pity the book was not widely read in its early years. Though a hodgepodge of various ideas,

Mein Kampf contained a terrible warning for Germany and the world. It clearly outlined the policies that Hitler intended to inaugurate if he ever came to power. Some historians feel that the Germans would not have permitted Hitler to rise as he did had they read the book and known what he had in mind for them.

In that mind were four basic ideas:

The Fuehrer Concept

First, to be great again, Germany must be ruled by a *Fuehrer*— a strong and dedicated leader, a leader with absolute authority. His word would be law and his orders would be carried out, without question or hesitation, by legions of subleaders throughout the nation. This system would insure that the country always moved ahead smoothly. There would never be the danger, as in a democracy, of such stumbling blocks and inefficiencies as dissenting opinions and actions.

The Master Race

The Fuehrer and all his subleaders would be of German descent. There would be no place in the scheme of things for the evil Jews and the peasant Slavs. The country had to be ruled by and for Germans because they were the modern children of an ancient and great race—the Aryans. As such, they alone had the physical strength and the intelligence to make the nation great.

The Aryans had peopled Europe and India in early times, and Hitler had developed the theory that everything fine in the world had come from them—all the best in culture, in music, in literature, in art, in law, and in science. But, through the centuries, they had allowed their magnificent strengths and talents to be weakened by mingling their blood with that of the inferior peoples around them. But today's pure Germans had remained free of that taint. They were still the Aryans of old. They were, in Hitler's words, a "master race" and the time had come for them to assert their superiority. They must join the Fuehrer in taking control of the country and rebuilding it.

Hitler wrote that the Aryans must never allow their blood to be tainted again. When he finally came to power, many of his policies were directed to this end. He outlawed marriages between "pure" Germans and the "inferiors" around them, especially the Jews. The various "non-Aryan" races in Germany—and then in the countries that Hitler subsequently invaded—were stripped of their wealth and their positions; they were replaced in their jobs by Germans and were imprisoned or made to work as slaves. As for that most hated of their lot—the Jew—the world soon learned of the horror that Hitler had in store for him.

The Lebensraum Plan

On two counts, Hitler envisioned an expanded Germany. First, the country must embrace *all* Germans, no matter where they lived. Just one interpretation could be given to this belief. Austria, Czechoslovakia, Poland, and Hungary all housed substantial German populations. Hitler intended to move against these countries and bring them under his thumb.

Second, he argued that Germany was so crowded that its people did not have sufficient *Lebensraum* (living space). Ample living space, of course, could be had only by expansion, and that expansion must be made eastward. There, vast stretches of open land for farming and settlement were to be found. The land Hitler was talking about lay in Russia.

The November Adventure

He prophesied that the eastward expansion would be easy. Russia had fallen into the hands of the Communists/Jews. They were incapable of maintaining a lasting government and had already weakened the country. Soon, they would bring Russia to a final collapse. Then those vast eastern lands would be there for the taking. The Germans could have them with little cost in blood to the master race.

The French Decision

Here, Hitler wrote that there must be a "final reckoning" with France. France, he said, had always been an implacable foe. She had always wanted a weak Germany, and the terms of the 1919 peace treaty showed that she was now out to have a "shattered and dismembered" Germany. And so, sooner or later, there must be a "last decisive struggle" between the two. Germany must defeat France, render her helpless, and see that she never became a danger again.

In all, for Germany and the entire world to see, *Mein Kampf* revealed Hitler's grand design for the future—a grand design for a totalitarianism that would brutalize and terrify the country and finally lead it into another world war.

But hardly anyone read the book. And the few who did either agreed with Hitler's plans or, just as tragically, failed to take him seriously.

The stage was being set for slaughter.

6. THE ROAD TO BERLIN

By DECEMBER, 1924, Hitler's influential friends had done their work well with the Bavarian authorities. The courts announced that Hitler had been a model prisoner and had learned his lesson. Further, the months spent in cell 7, away from the public eye, had cost him his political power. He could be safely paroled. Hitler walked out of Landsberg five days before Christmas.

Indeed, upon his release, Hitler was no longer a powerful man. In the wake of the putsch, the Bavarian government had outlawed the Nazi Party, forbidding it to hold private and public meetings. And, according to the terms of his parole, Hitler was not allowed to speak in public. Still worse, the NSDAP membership had fallen off drastically. Even some of his closest friends, certain that he had become a political "has-been," had fled to other organizations.

But, worst of all for him, the economic situation in Germany had changed during his Landsberg stay. The chaos and the runaway inflation of pre-putsch days had evaporated. This was due in great part to a series of loans (they would eventually add up to millions of dollars) being made to Germany by the Allied nations, especially Great Britain and the United States. They were doing wonders to stabilize the country's economy. In addition, the French had finally pulled out of the Ruhr and German industry was rolling again.

These developments had brought a sudden and welcome prosperity to the nation. After all the postwar years of struggle, there were jobs for practically everyone. New products were appearing on the market and old ones were returning. Businesses, large and small, were thriving. With full bellies and growing bank accounts, the people had little time for a politician whose message had been that the times were bad and that he was the one leader with the strength to make them good again.

But, no matter the prosperity, Hitler was determined to rebuild the NSDAP—and even more determined to put it on a national footing. In years past, he had always felt a sense of destiny. Now the putsch and the time in Landsberg had crystallized that sense. He now *knew* that he was a man of destiny, a man fated to lead his country one day.

It was a sense that gave him a new bearing. His friends quickly saw the change in him. In times past, he had been stiff and uncomfortable in the presence of his wealthy supporters; now he faced those still loyal to him with an assurance that said he saw himself as their equal. In times past, he had flown into rages when party business had gone wrong; now, though his temper was still volatile, he was better able to control himself, better able to face any problem with a cold and calculating quiet.

With his new-found calmness, Hitler made a decision that was to override all others for years to come. He would become Germany's leading political figure, yes, but he would reach his goal in a certain way. He had tried force on that terrible day in November and it had ended in disaster. He must never again use it against the government. It was too risky a way to seek power. From now on, he would work through legal channels and the ballot box. Force could be unleashed against such enemies as the Communists. But not the government. No matter how difficult things got to be in the next years.

Those next years were to be difficult ones indeed. The Nazi Party was to grow with agonizing slowness, first in secret and then openly when the ban on it was finally lifted. Only a few people joined its ranks. And those who did were not the best or the most stable to be found in Germany. Since the vast bulk of German workers, merchants, and professional people were content with life, Hitler attracted mainly the nation's malcontents, the ones who could not, or would not, prosper even in the best of times—the chronically unemployed, the outcasts, the rowdies, the failures who had to justify their failure by blaming it on the government.

Though it did so with agonizing slowness, the party did grow. Between 1926 and 1928, Hitler and his greatest helper at this time—a bluff and hearty man named Gregor Strasser—nursed its membership up to just over 100,000 nationwide. In the 1928 election for the Reichstag (the national parliament), the NSDAP received enough votes to send twelve representatives to the 491-member body. Yet Hitler always had to admit that his party was just about the smallest in the country. Those 1928 elections won his Nazis only 810,000 votes, a pitiful total when set against the fact that there were more than 31 million voters in Germany. Of all the parties represented in the Reichstag, his ranked a low ninth.

While he struggled with the problems of growth, Hitler made two new friends. He brought them close to him and, along with Hess and Goering, they eventually became major and feared Nazi figures. Their names were Paul Joseph Goebbels and Heinrich Himmler.

The son of working-class parents, Goebbels was a small, thin, black-haired man—*dwarfish* is the word that many historians have used to describe him. His head was abnormally large, as was his nose, and he had a tiny, receding chin. He walked with a severe limp, having been born with a clubfoot. At the time Hitler met him, Goebbels was a frustrated writer and a brilliant student who had studied philosophy, art, literature, and history at no fewer than six universities.

Goebbels started his Nazi career as the hearty Gregor Strasser's assistant. But he was quick to accept a job offer from Hitler, who saw a use for his writing talents. No sooner had Goebbels joined Hitler than he proved himself to be a tireless and devoted worker. He wrote speeches for his new boss, and newspaper releases and magazine articles for the party. He helped to arrange Nazi functions. In his devotion to a leader whom he thought to be a "political genius," Goebbels performed small personal services for Hitler and ran errands for him. His devotion was so doglike that he even began to imitate Hitler in manner and speech.

As for Hitler, he got a brilliant man who instinctively understood how to use the tools of propaganda to their fullest. Hitler would soon appoint him chief of the NSDAP's "cultural activities." As such, Goebbels would oversee the party's propaganda machinery and would eventually shape every creative endeavor in the country—from the most serious music and literature to the most popular magazines and films—to fit the Nazi cause.

Heinrich Himmler was Goebbels' opposite in many respects. He was a slender man of medium height who, though he was only in his late twenties, was beginning to go bald. To him went the appointment of commander of a newly formed party unit—the *Shutzstaffel* (guard detachment). It was a branch of the SA and was intended to serve as Hitler's private bodyguard; actually, it was a late outgrowth of the bodyguard unit that had been with him on the night he barged into the Buergerbrau-keller. Recruited to its ranks were tough and dedicated young men between the ages of eighteen and twenty-one; on signing up, they took an oath to sacrifice their lives for Hitler if necessary. In time, the *Shutzstaffel*—or SS, as it was most commonly known—served in a capacity far beyond its original function. During Hitler's years in power, Himmler developed it into a vast organizational network that ferreted out all "enemies of the state" and ran the infamous concentration camps that pocked the country like open sores.

To many Nazis, Hitler's choice of Himmler as the commander of the SS seemed an unlikely one. First, Himmler looked to be anything but a military man; rather, with his rimless glasses perched on a thin nose, he resembled a mild-mannered clerk. Second, he didn't come from a military background. A Bavarian by birth, Himmler had studied agriculture at the University of Munich, after which he had drifted through a variety of jobs—from bank teller to traveling salesman. He'd joined the NSDAP in the early 1920s and, at the time Hitler tapped him for the SS post, he was running a chicken ranch just to the west of Munich.

Party officials might criticize Hitler's choice, but he saw some characteristics behind Himmler's mild exterior that he knew would be valuable. There was a coldness and a cruelty there. And an icy hatred of everything non-German. And, perhaps most important of all, a deep belief in Hitler's view of the Germans as the world's "master race."

At about the time Hitler was gaining his two new friends, he broke with an old one—the scarred Ernst Roehm. The split resulted from a disagreement over how Roehm's SA should be used in the near future. Though the Nazi Party itself was small, the SA had swelled to a membership of 30,000 and Roehm, impatient at the slow way things were going, urged that it be marshaled for an armed takeover of the Republic. Hitler turned him down flat, insisting that the Nazis must now always work through legal channels. The whole matter ended in a violent quarrel, with the SA chief then resigning from the party. Roehm stalked off and went to South America, where he served for a time as an officer in the Bolivian army. He returned to Germany in 1930. Hitler, forgetting their argument in his old affection for the man, welcomed him back to the NSDAP and the SA's leadership.

The break with his good friend was a difficult one for Hitler. But it was as nothing when compared to the tragedy that befell him as the 1920s changed into the 1930s.

2.

The tragedy began to take shape in 1927, when Hitler rented a small villa in the mountains outside Munich. Ever since his release from Landsberg, he had lived in his usual frugal way, taking little or no money from the party and occupying his old bedroom apartment. But he had always managed to vacation in the surrounding mountains whenever possible and had come to love them. And so, when a wealthy party member offered to rent him the villa for just a few marks each month, he quickly accepted, moved in, and made the place his year-round home.

Just as quickly, he wrote to his half sister Angela, asking her to come and keep house for him. Angela had married a man named Leo Raubel many years earlier and had gone to Vienna with him. Raubel, however, was now dead. With no other opportunities in the offing, Angela decided to join Hitler. It was this decision that marked the real beginning of the tragedy.

Angela arrived at the villa with her daughter, Angela Maria—or Geli, as the family called her. Geli was twenty years old, an attractive girl whom Hitler's friends described as "charming" and "vivacious," though several later admitted to thinking her "coarse" and "flirtatious." Hitler, now approaching forty, was almost twice her age. But the difference in their years meant nothing to him. The man who seemed always uncomfortable in the presence of women—the man who had worshipped Stephanie Jansten from afar—promptly fell in love with his niece. And fell in love deeply.

Geli became Hitler's constant companion. He took her on long strolls in the woods. There were picnics and swimming parties with Nazi friends—though Hitler himself would never go near the water, insisting that no politician in his right mind should ever be seen or photographed in swimming trunks. Geli was at his side at party meetings in Munich, as she was at concerts, the opera, and the theater. Then in 1929, when Hitler was able to afford a large apartment in Munich, she went there to live with him.

At first, the affair amused his friends. His strange shyness of women was well known to them. But, in time, they came to see the romance as politically dangerous. It was not wise, they said, for him to be seen with a girl young enough to be his daughter. Nor was it wise for the two of them to be living together in the Munich apartment when not married; it was a situation bound to outrage the moral sense of many a voter. And it was certainly not wise of him to ignore party business, as he so often did, when Geli was nearby.

And, worse yet, the blood relationship was too close for comfort. Even though her mother was only Hitler's half sister, Geli was still his niece. If word of the close relationship was ever widely broadcast, it might well damage Hitler's reputation beyond repair.

On top of all else, there was the fact that the romance was anything but a happy one. Hitler was a jealous and possessive lover while Geli refused to be a timid and submissive young woman. Hitler wanted her all to himself, but she enjoyed flirting with the surrounding men. Once, Hitler suspected that Geli and his chauffeur were interested in each other. He attacked the man with a riding crop.

Geli also had ambitions for herself, ambitions that infuriated a man who thought she should devote all her attentions to him. The young woman had studied voice in Vienna at one time and wanted a career as a opera singer. Whenever she mentioned her desire to resume her lessons, a terrible argument would follow. She would pout for days and was not above locking herself in her room for all that time. Hitler would let party business slide until he managed a reconciliation.

The couple quarreled with particular violence over her opera career in 1931. A tearful Geli ended by saying that she was through with Hitler and was returning to her singing lessons in Vienna. Hitler shouted that she was forbidden to leave even the apartment. She was never to desert him. He stalked out and climbed into his Mercedes for a trip to a party meeting. He glanced up at Geli's window and saw her standing there, tears running down her face.

It was Hitler's last view of a living Geli. The next morning, she was found dead in her bedroom. A pistol lay alongside her body. It had been fired once. The bullet had entered her chest just below the shoulder and had pierced her heart.

The Bavarian authorities conducted an official investigation into the death. On the basis of the evidence studied, they listed it as suicide. There seemed to be no doubt, they said, that Fraulein Raubel's wound had been self-inflicted.

Hitler was devastated by Geli's death, as much so as he had been at the loss of his mother. He descended into one of his now-familiar moods of black depression. Party business went ignored. For a time, he would talk to no one. Several friends worried that he might take his own life. They later said that, throughout the rest of his years, Hitler could not mention Geli's name without tears coming to his eyes.

But, though his grief seemed real and deep, there were those friends who had their suspicions of Hitler. They knew that, in a fit of jealousy, his fury—which he now kept under such strict control—could erupt and become ungovernable. They wondered if he had returned to the apartment and, rekindling the argument, had so lost control of himself that he grabbed the pistol and fired the fatal shot.

And there was an even more widely held suspicion—that the bespectacled Heinrich Himmler had shot Geli or had ordered her murdered. Himmler was high among the party leaders who looked on the romance as so politically ruinous. For years, Munich could not rid itself of the rumor that Himmler had gotten the young woman out of the way so that she would not threaten Hitler's career at a time when he was finally coming into national prominence.

There is no evidence that Himmler was behind Geli's death. But there is also no question that by 1931, after years of struggling to rebuild the Nazi Party, Hitler had been catapulted to the forefront of the national scene. In fact, at the time of Geli's death, he was just ten months away from a momentous decision—the decision to run for President of Germany.

3.

The job of slowly rebuilding the party ended abruptly in 1929. Late that year, an economic depression, triggered by the crash of the American stock market, swept across the world. It hit Germany particularly hard. For all the good years, her economy had been much based on the loans from Great Britain and the United States, and now these countries, themselves terribly hard pressed, could make no more money available. Germany immediately went into a steep decline. Her industry slowed almost to a halt. Banks closed their doors for a time. Businesses and farms went bankrupt. In less than two years, 8 million Germans were jobless and facing starvation.

The situation was tailor-made for Hitler. He took full advantage of it. With the ban on his speaking in public long ago lifted, he threw himself into one speech after another. He blamed the depression on the greed of the capitalists. He accused the Weimar Republic of being too inept to make Germany prosperous again. He prophesied that the Communists would lure desperate workers to their ranks and try to take over the country. He ranted that the hated Jews, controlling so much of the world's wealth as they did, were somehow now making themselves even richer while countless Germans were starving. Only he and his Nazi Party had the wit and the strength to rescue the country.

As had happened back in the days of runaway inflation, an increasing number of people listened to his speeches and approved of what he was saying. And, as before, they began flocking to his party. They were not only terrified of starvation but were also at a loss to understand the complex forces that had caused the depression; it was good to hear a man who sounded as if he could lead them back to safety. Now, instead of growing a little each year, the NSDAP membership jumped by the hundreds, and then the thousands, each month.

While he captivated audiences with his speeches, Hitler also worked in private. He met with wealthy industrialists who were actually fattening themselves on the depression (they were doing so in great part by buying up property and bankrupt businesses for little or nothing and then holding them for future profit) and asked for their financial support. They had always suspected that his promise to institute a socialist state for the working classes had been a sham. Now he proved them right. He left no doubt that his current talk about capitalism being responsible for the depression was mere prattle to please the masses. He said that he would work to keep the nation's labor unions from becoming strong were he ever placed in power. And, of course, there was no question that he would seek to eliminate those perennial threats to capitalism—the Communists. Big business would always be favored by him.

That was all the industrialists needed to know. They began to pour money into the NSDAP treasury. Particularly heavy donations came from such men as Fritz Thyssen, the most powerful steel producer in the country; Emil Kirdorf, who was known as the Ruhr district's "coal king"; and Erhard Milch, technical director of the German airline, Lufthansa. With the funds, Hitler established magnificent Nazi headquarters in a former palace at Munich. And he used some of the money to rent the spacious apartment that he shared with Geli.

At the time the depression struck, the President of Germany was the stately—he stood six-feet-five-inches tall—and revered Field Marshal Paul von Hindenberg. Now in his early eighties, Hindenberg had been the supreme commander of the armed forces in the war and had occupied the presidency since 1925. A soldier rather than a politician and businessman, he was unable to stem the tide of the depression. Nor were the three Chancellors who served under him between 1929 and 1933. As each failed to do an ounce of good, Hindenberg was forced to try a replacement.

It is doubtful that anyone could have solved Germany's problems in those awful years. But, in great part, the Chancellors were prevented from doing so by the internal rivalries that had plagued the Reichstag since its inception. Not one of the many parties in the parliament yet held majority representation, and so there was no way of pushing through any program of helpful legislation. Whenever one party came up with what might have been some good ideas, its rivals, fearful of the prestige it might win, quickly killed them. Germany floundered like a rudderless ship.

Hitler's popularity grew apace with the worsening situation. In the parliamentary elections of 1930, he hoped that his Nazis would win at least fifty seats in the Reichstag, a jump of thirty-eight over the twelve previously held. But, when the election results were in, he was astonished and delighted to learn that his party had polled close to 6½ million votes. The Nazis were to have 107 representatives in the Reichstag. In just one day, the NSDAP had risen from its lowly ninth position and had become the second most powerful party in the land. Just ahead of it—but without a majority representation—was the Catholic Center Party.

As leader of the country's number-two party, Hitler now felt that he should be given the opportunity to try his hand at the Chancellorship. But Hindenberg appointed Charles Bruning to the job; Bruning headed the Catholic Center Party and had served as Chancellor prior to the election. For the next three years—years that saw Bruning replaced by two other men—Hitler insisted that he be given his chance. At every turn of the way, Hindenberg turned him down. Hindenberg said flatly that he wanted nothing to do with this "Bavarian upstart."

Hindenberg opposed Hitler on several counts. To begin, the old soldier took an instant dislike to him the first time they met. Hitler, who had been only a corporal in the war, was nervous in the presence of a Field Marshal and apparently talked too much to suit the President. After Hitler had left the room, Hindenberg turned to an aide and remarked sarcastically that the man was fit only to run some minor government department. He'd never make a proper Chancellor.

Further, Hindenberg didn't at all like one of the Nazi leader's political tactics. As Hitler had surged to prominence over the months, countless young men had joined the SA. By 1932, it was boasting close to 300,000 members. It not only guarded Hitler's public meetings, but had taken to attacking the meetings of rival parties, especially those of the hated Communists, who were rapidly gaining strength among Germany's desperate workers. There had been street fights. There had been injuries. And even deaths. Hindenberg refused to hand the Chancellorship to a man who sported his own private army and condoned such violence.

And he was appalled by a remark that Hitler, in a fit of sudden anger, made at one of their later meetings. Hitler said there was one way alone to end the growing Communist threat for once and all. Just give his Storm Troopers the freedom of the streets for three days. They'd root out the Communists wherever they found them. They'd have to kill at least 5,000 to get the job done. Hindenberg himself opposed the Communists. But this was talk of mass murder. It was insane.

Finally, there was undoubtedly more than a pinch of snobbery in Hindenberg's low regard of Hitler. The President was not only the country's highest-ranking military figure but was also a member of an old aristocratic family. He knew that Hitler came of peasant stock, had been a mere corporal in the war, and had once worked (or so it was rumored) as a house painter. In Hindenberg's view, Hitler's background was too humble for the demands and responsibilities of the Chancellorship.

Germany's next presidential and parliamentary elections fell due in 1932. Early in the year, Hindenberg announced his intention to stand for another term as President. By now, Paul Joseph Goebbels had become one of Hitler's closest advisors and he argued that the NSDAP, with all its new-won strength, should field an opposing candidate. He urged Hitler to run. But Hitler at first shook his head and then agreed only with great reluctance. His reluctance didn't stem from any affection for the man who had so insistently thwarted his ambitions. Rather, he felt that Hindenberg, though now eighty-five, would be too tough to beat. No matter the sorry state of German affairs, the old soldier was still one of the most respected men in the country.

"I see myself as Chancellor and I will be Chancellor," he told his friends at one point. "I do not see myself as President and I know that I will never be President."

He was right—at least, for the moment. Though staging an ambitious campaign that took him to all parts of the country, the Nazi leader ran a poor second to Hindenberg when the ballots were counted on April 10. Hindenberg polled 19,359,983 votes—or 53 percent of the electorate. Hitler drew 13,418,547 votes for a 36.8 percent share. A third candidate, Ernst Thaelman of the Communist Party, received 3,706,759 votes.

The elections did, however, solve one problem for Hitler. Ever since leaving Vienna and settling in Munich, he had wanted to become a German citizen. It was an embarrassment—and a drawback—not to be a citizen of the country he hoped to lead. But there had never seemed to be enough free time to resolve the matter. Now, planning to run for President, he could delay no longer. The Weimar constitution admitted only German citizens to the presidency.

Sidestepping all the formalities and preparations that the process customarily involved, Hitler became a German citizen on February 26, 1932. He did so with the help of a fellow Nazi who also happened to be Germany's Minister of the Interior. The minister appointed him to an official position in the state of Brunswick. The position automatically made Hitler a citizen of the state and, thus, of Germany. He announced his presidential candidacy the next day.

Though himself defeated in the elections, Hitler saw them as a triumph for his party. They brought an additional 123 Nazis to the Reichstag. The NSDAP, with a grand total of 230 seats to its credit, now ranked as the number-one party in the country. But Hitler had to admit that the triumph was a limited one because the elections did not give the NSDAP a clear-cut majority there. And so it was easy for Hindenberg to overlook him and reappoint as Chancellor the man who had replaced Bruning sometime earlier—the aristocratic Franz von Papen.

The country remained a rudderless ship. Von Papen could do nothing to improve matters, and confusion continued to reign in the Reichstag, with the rival parties constantly warring among themselves. Desperate for some solution to the mess, Hindenberg dismissed von Papen in December of the year and replaced him with a close aide, General Kurt von Schleicher.

There was turmoil outside the government as well as within during the months of von Papen's Chancellorship. Jobless workers were demonstrating for help. Employed workers had been made to accept reduced wages and were striking for better pay. And the SA and the Communists, now vicious rivals, were battling in the streets. In June alone, there were more than 450 clashes between the two in the state of Prussia. Some 400 men were injured and eighty-two were killed. In July, when the SA staged a great parade in the city of Hamburg, the Communists attacked. Nineteen people, from both sides, were shot dead in the streets. More than 280 sustained wounds.

By now, the monumental size of the SA worried many Germans. They feared that Hitler, so long frustrated in his bid for the Chancellorship, might take it into his head to grab the government by force with this awesome private army. Their fear changed the lives of many Germans. For safety's sake, they flocked to the party in greater numbers than ever. People who had voiced a dislike of Hitler just a few weeks—or even a few days—ago could now be seen wearing swastika armbands. Many began to shun their Jewish friends. Some dissolved their business associations with Jews. Some even went so far as to divorce their Jewish spouses.

In fairness, it must be stressed that not all Germans took these steps. Just as many refused to side with Hitler. And just as many remained loyal to their Jewish friends, associates, and loved ones. They were certain that Hitler's anti-Semitic outbursts were nothing more than the empty, though assuredly foul, mouthings of an ambitious politician; once he got what he wanted, his common sense would take over. Further, Germany was a civilized nation and would never allow the persecution and annihilation of millions of its people. It was unthinkable.

As for the Jews themselves, countless of their number agreed with this view. In addition, many looked on themselves not only as Jews—or not as Jews at all—but as Germans. Surely, as loyal Germans, they would be safe. Oh, their lives might be made uncomfortable for a while. But they would be fine in the long run. A few Jews, however, took Hitler with dead seriousness. They began to leave the country. They were the lucky ones.

Hitler, of course, had no intention of storming the government with his SA, no matter what the people thought. Rather, he spent the remainder of 1932 pressing Hindenberg for the Chancellorship. As always, his efforts went for nothing. Then, in January, 1933, his fortunes suddenly changed.

The recently appointed Chancellor, General Kurt von Schleicher, triggered the change when he approached Hindenberg with a request. He said that the perennial confusion in the Reichstag was making it impossible for him to be an effective Chancellor. There was only one way left for him to lead the country. The President must allow him to take advantage of the "emergency powers" clause in the Weimar constitution. These were powers reserved for use in a dire emergency. They would permit Schleicher to govern by decree rather than via democratic action in the parliament. Using them, Schleicher wanted to dissolve the Reichstag and establish a military dictatorship. There would then be no one to hamper his efforts to save the country.

A military dictatorship? Though a professional soldier himself, Hindenberg shook his head. He knew that even the thought of it would create havoc everywhere. It would enrage all those who, whether they were for or against the Weimar Republic, would not tolerate life under the thumb of the military. And it would enrage all those—especially the Communists and Hitler's Nazis—who were willing to see the Republic destroyed but who wouldn't settle for seeing it replaced with any leadership but their own. The result could be civil war.

No, Schleicher must go on trying to work with the Reichstag. Schleicher replied that the President was asking the impossible. Hindenberg was, he concluded, leaving him with but one alternative—to think about resigning. The President nodded coldly.

With that, the Chancellor stalked out of the room. Hindenberg began immediately to cast about for a replacement, knowing all the while that Hitler was his last remaining choice.

Then his son and aide, Major Oskar von Hindenberg, said that Hitler would make a good Chancellor. This was an opinion that would have startled the President in times past. Oskar had always shared his father's intense dislike of Hitler—that is, until early this January when he met in private with the Nazi leader for a talk about the Chancellorship. No one knew what was said in that meeting, but somehow, in the space of an hour or so, Hitler had transformed Oskar into one of his most outspoken supporters. Now Hindenberg responded to his son's remark by calling Hitler to the Presidential Palace. It was the action of a defeated man. At eighty-five, he suddenly felt so very tired . . .

Berlin was a tense city on the gray morning of January 30, 1933, when Hitler and the men who would be his cabinet ministers arrived at the Palace. News of the Nazi leader's imminent appointment had spread to every neighborhood. General Schleicher had reacted in a blind rage and had threatened to lead the army in a takeover of the government if Hitler actually became Chancellor. It was an empty threat—Schleicher simply didn't have the influence to make it good—but Hitler had taken no chances. He had alerted the SA in Berlin to stand by to repulse any attack; Storm Troopers from all over the country were flooding into the city to lend a hand if necessary. In the streets, there was the heavy, charged silence that comes when people know they're sitting on a lighted powder keg.

Hitler and his intended cabinet ministers entered the anteroom adjoining Hindenberg's office at midmorning. They were kept waiting there, nervous and perspiring, for long minutes. At 11:15, an aide escorted them into Hindenberg's presence. The Field Marshal looked very old and pale. He was leaning heavily on a cane.

It was customary for a President to welcome the incoming Chancellor and formally tell him of his appointment. But Hindenberg couldn't bring himself to do so. Nor did he greet the cabinet ministers. He did no more than conduct the simple swearing-in ceremony. Then he stood by, his face a hard mask, while Hitler gave a short speech in which he promised to support the Republic and return Germany to economic stability. On finishing, he waited for some reciprocal remarks from Hindenberg. But there were none. Hindenberg merely said, "And now, gentlemen, forward with God." He limped from the room.

In the moment of his greatest triumph, Hitler was left standing there with his ministers. Several of the men felt as if they were soldiers who had just been haughtily dismissed after a session of close-order drill. Swallowing his anger at the slight, Hitler led the way out, only to realize that he had hired a photographer for the occasion and then had forgotten to have him take some pictures. He went immediately to his Berlin headquarters. There, with delirious supporters and friends swarming all around, he was able to smile again and shout with glee, "We've done it! We've done it!"

Indeed, he had done it. He'd finally achieved the power he had sought for so long. But, in the same instant, he knew that his appointment was held in place by the most delicate of threads. Hindenberg could cut that thread at any moment he chose, in any moment of anger or dislike.

Something must now be done to make that thread unbreakable. And it must be done immediately.

7. POWER AND DEATH

WITHIN HOURS AFTER his appointment, Hitler's supporters were staging one of the greatest celebrations ever seen in Berlin. More than 25,000 SA and SS troopers came together at the Tiergarten, a large park near the heart of the city. From there, as night closed down, they marched along the wide boulevard that flowed past the main government buildings. Behind them walked thousands of party members in civilian dress.

As the marchers strode beneath the main balcony of the Presidential Palace, they respectfully saluted the stately Paul von Hindenberg. But moments later, when abreast of the Chancellory building, they began to cheer wildly. For there, standing in the open window of his new office, was Hitler. His face was flushed. He could be seen moving up and down, as though skipping in place in his excitement. Behind him were his chief aides—the mountainous Goering, the spiderlike Goebbels, and the thin Hess and Himmler.

Rolling in above the cheers like thunder were the marchers' repeated chants of "Heil Hitler." It was the ceremonial greeting used by all party members and had been invented by Hitler sometime after he designed the Nazi flag. One of his tactics for imbuing his followers with a sense of pageantry, it was not an original invention but had been borrowed from the old Roman cry, "Hail Caesar." Also borrowed from the Romans was the Nazi salute—a stiffly upraised arm with hand outstretched.

The parade below was the work of Goebbels. He had spent the afternoon summoning and organizing the marchers. They all carried flaming torches that turned the boulevard into a river of fire. At one point, a very impressed Hitler turned to Goebbels and asked, "Where did you find all those torches?" All that he got in reply was a satisfied smile.

Even as he watched the parade, Hitler was thinking of what he could do to strengthen his position as Chancellor. He knew that real power would never be his until the Nazis held a majority representation in the Reichstag. Only with their majority votes could he push legislation past the rival parties—legislation that would eventually make his word law.

A majority in the Reichstag could be achieved in just one way—through the ballot box. But he didn't have the time to wait for the next regular elections some two years from now. He must arrange for an immediate special election and then stage a campaign that would win his Nazis an overwhelming victory. But special elections were hard to come by. They were held only if a current parliament failed to do its job and was dissolved by the President.

Hitler decided on a two-move strategy to get the election. First, in early February, he summoned the leaders of every party in the Reichstag to a meeting. The new Chancellor asked them to cooperate with him in shaping a program to rebuild

Germany and then made certain that the session ended in chaos, after which it was time for his second move. Off to Hindenberg's office he rushed. There, describing how the parties had failed to work together when given such a fine chance, he demanded that the President dissolve the Reichstag so that a more unified replacement could be found.

It was a risky demand that could have resulted in the President dismissing him as Chancellor. He knew that Hindenberg would be against a special election on the grounds that it might add to the turmoil already in the country. But, as he had hoped, the old man was too tired these days to argue; Hitler even noted that his mind seemed to wander at times. Hindenberg decreed that the Reichstag be dissolved. The special election would be held on the coming March 5.

Working with fanatical intensity, Hitler and Goebbels threw themselves into a stunning, month-long campaign for votes. Hitler went first to his industrialist friends and got them to contribute 3 million marks to the effort. Then, climbing aboard a plane and enduring the airsickness that often bothered him, he embarked on a speaking tour for the Nazi candidates who were springing up everywhere. Between speeches, he made nationwide radio broadcasts arranged by Goebbels; it was the first time in German history that radio played an important role in electioneering. For families who did not own radios, Goebbels had loudspeakers set up in shops and on street corners. The little man also outfitted trucks with public address systems and sent them cruising about with messages from the NSDAP. Almost daily, he staged party meetings, rallies, and parades.

But there was a problem—and both Hitler and Goebbels recognized it. As would be true in any election, they had no guarantee of winning the overwhelming victory they needed for a Reichstag majority, no matter how energetic a campaign they waged. For that kind of win, they required an issue of staggering import, one that would bring voters flocking to the Nazis in greater numbers than ever before. Hitler met with his party leaders to discuss the problem. Out of the session came a scheme against their longtime enemies, the Communists.

The Communists were campaigning just as vigorously as the Nazis. The scheme called for the word to be spread that, as they campaigned, the Reds were plotting a massive revolution; if successful, it would place Germany in the hands of their Russian masters. Goebbels started things off with a radio broadcast. Hitler followed with ranting speeches in which he claimed that he alone, backed by a Nazi-dominated Reichstag, could stop the Reds. The SA began attacking Communist meetings on the pretext of quelling the trouble before it started. And Goering himself led a raid on the Communist Party headquarters in Berlin. He came away claiming that he had found "official documents" outlining the planned revolt.

But, in great part because Goering refused to make the documents public (he couldn't without proving himself a liar, since they were really nothing more than old propaganda pamphlets), the scheme fell flat on its face. Most voters recognized it as a clumsy political trick. Hitler was deeply embarrassed.

But his embarrassment lasted just a short time—until flames lighted the Berlin sky on the night of February 27.

2.

Hitler arrived at Goebbels' apartment early that evening for a small dinner party. A few hours later, as he sat listening to phonograph records with his host and several associates, the telephone rang in the outer hallway. Goebbels answered it and heard a breathless friend say that the building housing the Reichstag was on fire.

At first, as Goebbels later wrote in his diary, he did not

believe the news and decided not to bother Hitler with it. Then he had second thoughts. He picked up the telephone, dialed several friends, and had the frightening truth confirmed. Some said that they could see smoke and a red glow in the sky. Others could see the dome of the giant building; flames were bursting from it.

On hearing the news, Hitler jumped to his feet and, as Goebbels wrote, "We raced like mad through the streets." The sight that greeted them on their arrival stunned them. Flames were shooting from the building's upper windows and from beneath the great dome. Firemen had the place surrounded. They had already put out the fire in the vast entrance hall. The hall was a smoking ruins.

Hitler pushed his way into the hall, followed by a group of Nazi officials and foreign correspondents who had gathered outside. There, he met a puffing, red-faced Hermann Goering. Goering had been a member of the parliament and had been serving as its presiding officer at the time it was dissolved; as such, he occupied an official residence next door. He'd rushed over as soon as he had sighted the flames, and now he greeted the Hitler group with the word that the fire had not been accidental but had been deliberately set.

Face flushed, he told one Nazi friend, "This is the beginning of the Communist revolution. We must not wait a minute. We will show them no mercy. Every Communist official must be shot where he is found. Every Communist this night must be strung up."

Puffing and excited though he was, Goering hadn't forgotten the Nazi scheme. Not for a moment.

He then informed Hitler that the man who had set the fire had already been captured. The arsonist turned out to be a young, half-demented Dutchman named Marinus van der Lubbe. Back home, he had been a member of a small extremist group of Communists. He hated capitalism and had a history of making political protests by setting fire to public buildings. It was later learned that van der Lubbe had arrived in Berlin a few days earlier and had been heard to boast that he intended to put the torch to the Reichstag building. He had been caught while still inside the place.

All this was welcome news to Hitler. So the arsonist was a Red, was he? Perfect! The fool had given him just what was needed to salvage the Nazi scheme. The fire could be broadcast as the start of the Communist uprising. Then, when the revolution failed to materialize, it could still stand as a deliberate Red plot against a government building rather than an isolated instance of arson. Either way, it played right into his hands.

Hitler remained at the burning building throughout the night, watching it reduce itself to a mass of charred rubble and twisted, blackened girders. He said that van der Lubbe must be brought to trial immediately, with all attendant publicity. He told Goebbels to get the news of the fire on the radio immediately. Goebbels must announce that it marked the start of the uprising and that more public buildings were certain to be soon torched. Goebbels nodded. He knew what to do.

Many Germans bought Goebbels' propaganda when it was broadcast. But just as many did not. In the next days, a suspicion grew throughout the country—and, indeed, the world—that the Nazis themselves had fired the Reichstag so that they could blame it on the Communists. The suspicion took shape when an investigation revealed that the fire had been started with gasoline and in several places. It seemed to many Germans that one man alone could not have carried enough fuel to get the job done. Several men would have been needed. But no one but van der Lubbe had been captured. Nor had anyone else been seen escaping from the building.

Then came a news report of a tunnel that ran to the basement of the Reichstag from beneath Goering's official residence next door. It was meant to house central heating pipes for the two buildings. People immediately realized how, without ever being detected, a group of Storm Troopers could have carried cans of gasoline along the tunnel and then made a quick escape back through it.

To this day, the full truth behind the fire remains unknown. Van der Lubbe went on trial in 1934; tried with him were three Communist leaders whom the Nazis accused of being his co-conspirators. Throughout the trial, van der Lubbe insisted that he had worked alone. When no solid evidence could be brought against the three leaders, they were acquitted. The court found van der Lubbe guilty and sentenced him to death. He was executed by decapitation.

Years later, a second and more thorough investigation was made of the fire. The evidence pointed the finger of blame at the Nazis. It indicated that, indeed, a band of Storm Troopers had made their way through the tunnel. But even then a question remained: how did they know that van der Lubbe would be in the Reichstag on that very night? The answer seems to be that the SA had heard him speak of his plans some days earlier and had taken him briefly into custody. At that time, they may have learned the date of his planned strike or may have planted a certain date in his mind. Or, after releasing him, they may have kept him under surveillance until they were certain of when he planned to enter the Reichstag.

(In late 1980, a West Berlin court overturned the verdict against van der Lubbe on the grounds that, indeed, he had been the "weak-willed" tool of the Nazis. His brother had attempted to have the verdict reduced since 1955, but had succeeded only in having the sentenced reduced posthumously from death to a prison term.)

The suspicion has always been that the fire was the brainchild

107

of Goebbels and Goering. In fact, there's a story that Goering, during a birthday party for Hitler some years later, slapped his knee with a great flat hand and boasted, "I set the fire." Officially, though, he always claimed that he had nothing to do with it.

There seems little doubt that Hitler himself was *not* in on the plot. For one thing, he seemed genuinely appalled when he reached the building and saw it wrapped in flames. For another, he turned to a foreign correspondent on the scene and blurted, "God grant that this be the work of the Communists." Unless he was doing a fine bit of play-acting, everything indicates that he had no prior knowledge of the blaze.

3.

Whether he was in on the conspiracy or not, Hitler took full advantage of the fire. It enabled him to bolster his scheme against the Communists with a new plot, one that he sneaked across on von Hindenberg when he went to the President with an account of the disaster.

Insisting that the fire signaled the beginning of the Red uprising, he brought with him a presidential decree for Hindenberg to sign. Hitler said that the decree, which was titled "For the Protection of the People and the State," would give him the authority as Chancellor to take whatever steps were necessary to crush the revolt. The President must sign it if Germany was to be safeguarded against the next Communist moves. The old man, more weary than ever of the ills besetting the country, reached for his pen.

The wording of the decree called for it to remain in effect until the threat of the revolt passed. It was a harsh document. What it did was cancel all individual and civil rights granted to citizens under the Weimar constitution. Cancelled were the rights of free expression, free assembly, and a free press. Houses and buildings could be searched without a warrant. Property could be seized without an argument.

In addition, the "Reichstag fire decree," as many Germans soon christened it, empowered the central government to take control in any state where trouble erupted. Finally, it imposed the death penalty on any armed person who "seriously disturbed the peace."

As he had planned it would, the decree placed in Hitler's hands a terrible weapon that Hindenberg did not see—or chose to ignore in his weariness. It not only permitted the Chancellor to move against the Communists. It also freed him to move against *any* opposition party under the guise of putting down the revolt. And so it was with an effort that he masked his delight as the presidential signature was put to the decree. His long-standing pledge to work always through legal channels had been especially difficult to keep during an election that meant so much to his future. He had already allowed the SA to use some force against the Communists. But now he had the power—the legal power—to hit all the parties and crush them completely. His Nazis could be sure of a majority in the Reichstag.

In the next days, Hitler put the cruelest of his old Vienna techniques—that of raw terror—to work. Swarms of brown-shirted SA troopers, charging through the streets in trucks, descended on political meetings everywhere. The crowds were dispersed. Anyone who resisted was set to flight with clubs and rifle butts. Speakers were dragged from rostrums and thrown into trucks for the trip to jail. Of all the targets, the Communists were, of course, the hardest hit. More than 4,000 Communist leaders and members were arrested and hauled off to SA barracks, where they were imprisoned for days, beaten, and often tortured. All the while, the police stood by helplessly and watched the mayhem. Chancellor Hitler was working within the law, quelling a Red uprising. There was nothing they could do to intervene.

While the Storm Troopers did their work, propagandist Paul Joseph Goebbels did his. He continued to treat Germany to the most intense political campaign it had ever witnessed. He went on swamping the radio with speeches by Hitler, Goering, and himself. His trucks and their public-address systems were everywhere. So were his legions of helpers who joined the SA in tearing down opposition posters and replacing them with red-and-black Nazi ones. He raised the swastika above public buildings throughout the country. At night, he continually reminded the people of the Nazi cause by lighting great bonfires on the hillsides ringing their towns and cities.

And how did all the work end on March 5? Millions of Germans, cowed by Hitler's terror tactics or impressed by the intensity of the campaign, entrusted their votes to the Nazis. But just as many millions, disgusted by all they had seen, declared that they wanted no part of the Chancellor and his people.

The election of March 5, 1933, was the last democratic one that Germany was to see in Hitler's lifetime. When the ballots were counted, the Nazis led all the opposition parties with 17,277,180 votes. The Social Democratic Party polled just over 7 million. The Catholic Center Party, the former leader, came in with close to 5 million. So did the Communist Party.

On the surface, the results looked good for Hitler. The votes made his NSDAP again the number-one party in the land. But, beneath the surface, there was sharp disappointment because those 17 million votes represented less than half the current German electorate and sent only 288 Nazis to the Reichstag. Hitler had not won the majority representation that he wanted.

But he was too far along the road to full power to be turned back by disappointing election results. So the strategy of a special election had failed, had it? All right. He would replace it with a new strategy. He would still have his majority representation.

4.

Hitler launched the strategy by facing the public as a triumphant Chancellor. He claimed that the election had been a mighty victory for the Nazi Party. In fact, it had been more than a victory; it had been a "revolution" by the German voters. With their ballots, they had said that they wanted to cast off the old. They wanted a new kind of government. *His* kind of government. He would grant them their wish when the new parliament met for the first time.

With the Reichstag building still a smouldering ruin, the infant parliament assembled at Berlin's Kroll Opera House in mid-March for that first meeting. Hitler immediately mounted the stage and unveiled his new strategy. He bluntly told the members that he wanted them to pass what he called an "enabling act."

It was a demand that stunned the representatives in the opposition ranks. The measure, which was formally titled the "Law for Removing the Distress of the German People and the Reich," called for the Reichstag to give up its constitutional powers—its powers to make laws—for a period of four years (Hitler had no intention of *ever* returning them). Those powers were to be placed in the hands of the Chancellor and his cabinet.

Arguing with all the passion he could summon, Hitler said that past parliaments had never been able to forget party rivalries and pass legislation that would lead Germany out of her many troubles. Now this Reichstag must show good sense and enable him to develop and enact the needed laws himself. It was the only way to give the country quick and decisive action. He assured his listeners that he wouldn't misuse the powers given him. After all, he would still be answerable to President von Hindenberg.

To be enacted, the measure would require a two-thirds favorable vote. From the shocked and pale faces below him, Hitler knew that his opponents had no intention of going along with him. Regardless of what he said about von Hindenberg, they knew he was asking for the powers of a dictator. It was an impossible demand in a Republic.

Hitler ended his speech and requested that the measure be brought up for a vote on March 23. Then, as he had all along known he would do, he set out to break his uncooperative opponents. He did so in a ruthless fashion, starting with a fresh attack on the Communists—this time, the Communist representatives in the Reichstag.

The Communist Party had managed to place about 100 representatives in the parliament. Using the fire decree as his legal means, Hitler accused the party of a new plot against the government and ordered the representatives arrested and jailed; they were sitting in their cells, safely out of the action, when the act came up for its vote. Next, on the day of the vote, he stationed SA guards at the opera house entrance and had them refuse admission to a number of Social Democrat representatives on various trumped-up "technical grounds." That day, he also tricked the members of yet another opposition party into a favorable vote by agreeing to give them a written promise never to abuse the powers granted him; somehow, he managed never to write and deliver the promise. Finally, he stationed SA toughs throughout the auditorium, their obvious task being to frighten his remaining enemies into "yes" votes.

His tactics worked. Of the members who made their way into the Kroll Opera House that March 23, 441 voted in favor of the enabling act. There were a scant 94 courageous "nay" votes.

Armed now with the enabling act and the fire decree, Hitler's political power was almost absolute. Of all the men in the country, he was answerable to just one—von Hindenberg. But he wasn't much worried about the old man. The President, now eighty-five, with his health continuing to fail and his mind wandering more and more, couldn't possibly have the strength to oppose whatever laws he now enacted. Nor could Germany expect her President to live too much longer.

Hitler remembered how, on the night of his appointment as Chancellor, he had set out to strengthen his newly won position. Well, he had done so, far beyond his greatest expectations that night, and he had done so with astonishing speed. It seemed hardly possible that not even two months had passed since he had stood watching his Storm Troopers turn the boulevard below his window into a river of fire with all those torches that Goebbels had miraculously provided.

As soon as the enabling act was passed, Hitler proclaimed the end of the Weimar Republic. It was just thirteen years old at the time of its death. He announced the birth of the Third Reich.

Just what did Hitler mean by Third Reich? In general, the word *reich* means "state" and has come specifically to mean "German state." In Hitler's view, the original Holy Roman Empire of German States (founded in A.D. 800) constituted the First Reich. The Second Reich, he argued, existed from the early 1800s until the founding of the Weimar Republic. His regime, then, marked the beginning of the Third Reich.

He boasted that he would build such a strong Germany that this Third Reich would endure for "a thousand years." History was to prove him tragically wrong.

Hitler spent the next months laying the foundation for that

greater Germany and increasing his own strength even more. First, he started to bring the various German states under his control by enacting a law that installed Nazi officials as their governors. Then, a short time later, he completed the job with a second law; it killed the state parliaments and transferred all state powers to the central government. The states found themselves no longer independent entities but mere arms of the central government. Their Nazi governors were pledged to carry out at all times "the policies laid down by the Reich Chancellor." The Fuehrer concept—the idea of the unquestioned leader supported by the all-obedient subleaders—that had been voiced in *Mein Kampf* was now being put into practice.

Next, to the delight of his industrialist backers, he took over the nation's labor unions. Appointed as their heads were Nazi officials. The Chancellor announced that, for the sake of increasing Germany's production, workers were now forbidden to strike and were required at all times to obey the orders of their bosses and new union leaders.

While making these moves, he turned again on the opposition parties in the Reichstag. Even with the immense powers of the enabling act, Hitler was worried that his opponents might somehow still rise to block his way. He had already put the Communist representatives out of business by jailing them and he now set out to dispose of his remaining enemies. The Social Democrats were his first victims. Goering and the police seized their offices throughout the country and confiscated their treasury. In June, again waving the fire decree in the public's face, Hitler declared the Social Democrats to be "subversive and inimical to the state." Many of their leaders were jailed. Some managed to go underground or flee the country.

In the face of these terror tactics, the other parties began dissolving themselves. By July, they were all gone. One party alone remained in the Reichstag—the NSDAP. Hitler then announced the passage of yet another law. It bluntly declared that "the National Socialist German Workers Party constitutes the only political party in Germany." It further stated that anyone who tried to "form" or "maintain" another party would be slapped in prison for three months to five years.

From that day to the end of Hitler's life, all German elections for the Reichstag saw only Nazi candidates. There was never again in the parliament a single voice to speak up against his dictates.

5.

Oddly enough, all the while that Hitler was tightening his grip on Germany in 1933 and then 1934, he was up against trouble inside the NSDAP. It came, as it had once before, from the scarred Ernst Roehm. The two men had angrily separated back in the 1920s and Roehm had gone to South America for a time. He had returned to Germany and the Nazi cause in the 1930s. Now, as before, he was chief of the SA.

And he was as ambitious as ever. The SA had grown to a membership of more than 2 million brown-shirted men; it was twenty times larger than the 100,000-man army dictated by the Treaty of Versailles. Roehm felt—and he made no secret of his opinion—that the SA should be named the major military force in the country, with the army and navy subordinate to it. Further, he felt that all military forces should be placed under a single Minister of Defense. He, of course, should be appointed as that Minister.

Hitler thought the whole idea ridiculous and rejected it out of hand. He knew that the generals and the admirals would never stand still for it. They would never want their forces to play second fiddle to anyone. Nor would they ever serve under Roehm. It was widely known that, despite his tough

115

manner and hard face, he was a homosexual and was surrounded by homosexual aides. The armed services of the country, their leaders said, must never be entrusted to such a man.

Roehm's idea may have struck Hitler as ridiculous, but he found the trouble it might cause unnerving. So far, the generals and the admirals, though he knew that many shared President von Hindenberg's low opinion of him, had done nothing to oppose his march to power. But, if they ever decided to do so, ever decided to rebel and throw their men against his, he could be in the worst trouble possible. In the end, he might well win, but his regime could be so torn asunder that he'd never again be truly powerful. Roehm's stupid insistence on being Defense Minister was the exact spark needed to ignite a military uprising.

Hitler, of course, had the authority to dismiss Roehm from his SA command and the party. But he dared not use it. Roehm was revered by his Storm Troopers and such an action might well trigger quite another rebellion. Further, Hitler could not forget his own liking of the man. Their personal friendship persisted despite the friction between them.

The situation came to a head in 1934. In the spring of that year, a rumor went through Berlin. It held that Roehm had finally tired of having his aims for the SA and himself turned down. He had gathered some of his top SA officers together and had hatched a plot to overthrow the Nazi regime; also said to be in on the plot were several prominent army officers, chief among them General Kurt von Schleicher, the former Chancellor. If the rumor was to be believed, Roehm planned to have the SA seize the city and take Hitler prisoner.

The rumor triggered panic. Frail as he was, President von Hindenberg roused himself and summoned Hitler to the Presidential Palace. He told the Chancellor to put an immediate end to the plot; the country could not stand the emotional strain of another upheaval. Restore quiet, he instructed. Bring the SA under control. Or, regardless of Hitler's power, the President would dismiss him as Chancellor, declare martial law, and hand the nation over to the army and navy.

The old man's threat struck Hitler like a physical blow. To fight the dismissal he'd have to defy the President. And that could lead to open warfare with the armed forces. It could be as disastrous as the military uprising he so feared.

To this day, it is not known whether Roehm actually did hatch a plot to overthrow Hitler. Many historians believe that, again, the fine hand of Goering can be seen, along with that of Heinrich Himmler. Both men hated Roehm and wanted to see him out of the way. And both hated the power he was seeking. It was a threat to their own. What better reason for them to dream up the plot themselves and then spread the rumor?

But there can be no question on one point. Hitler believed the rumor. He was hurt and furious at his old friend's treachery. He was in near hysteria over the threat of martial law. And so he was in the mood to listen when he met with Goering and Himmler after receiving Hindenberg's ultimatum. They told him that he must strike immediately. He must arrest Roehm and all the SA men close to him; they must be stamped out as if they were poisonous spiders. And, at the same time, he must eliminate all his other enemies—all those who, inside and outside the party, were still against him. Only then could he be safe to lead the country. Hitler nodded. His face was ashen. There was still a part of him that hated to destroy Roehm. But he agreed to handle the SA chief while Goering took care of all the "other enemies."

The last day of June, 1934, was set as the date for what became known as the "blood purge." At that time, Roehm and a number of his closest friends were vacationing at the Han-

117

slbauer Hotel on the shores of a lake near Munich. A vacation was hardly something that a man plotting a Chancellor's over-throw would take, but Hitler didn't think of that as, with Goeb-bels, he boarded a trimotor Junkers for the flight to Bavaria.

The plane took off at two in the morning and landed at Munich just before dawn. Accompanied by a band of local police officers, Hitler immediately arrested several SA leaders known to be friendly to Roehm. He gave the captives no chance to speak, but sent them off to Stadelheim Prison. Then, com-mandeering several automobiles, the Chancellor and his party sped to the Hanslbauer. They pulled up at its front entrance just as the sun was rising.

Roehm's friends were all asleep. They were awakened by quiet knocks at their doors. On answering, they found them-selves staring into pistol and rifle barrels. Again, no one was given the chance to speak. Everyone was instructed to dress. Then the prisoners were herded into a laundry room, there to await two buses for the return to Munich and Stadelheim. They were told nothing more than that they were under arrest for treason.

Hitler himself, wearing a leather trench coat and carrying a pistol, went to Roehm's room. He was obviously nervous— a combination of fury at the SA chief and hatred of what he must now do to an old friend. A police officer knocked on the door for Hitler. Then, without waiting for an answer, Hitler pushed his way into the room. He crossed to the bed. Roehm, his scarred face dazed with sleep, looked up at him.

Hitler forced himself to control his storming emotions. The accompanying police officer always remembered him as tense but quiet. Calling Roehm by his first name, Hitler informed him that he was under arrest. He accused him of being a traitor to his Fuehrer, his party, his country. He instructed Roehm to dress. Then he spun on his heel and walked out. Roehm tried to protest his innocence. But Hitler was gone.

Roehm and his friends were in Stadelheim Prison by late morning. Hitler, now so nervous that one policeman later said he was actually foaming at the mouth, sat down with a list of the prisoners' names. He checked off a half-dozen names (some reports say a dozen). They were those of the men who seemed closest to Roehm. Hitler ordered that the designated six be executed immediately.

A high-ranking Nazi who had arrived on the scene from his Munich home protested the order. It wasn't legal, he argued, to execute the prisoners without a trial. Hitler would damage his reputation if he didn't remain within the bounds of the law. The man who had long insisted on working through legal channels now screamed that the prisoners were "criminals against the Reich." They must die. Now!

And so the killings began. Throughout the late afternoon and then the evening, the doomed men were marched, one at a time, into the prison courtyard and placed in front of a firing squad of SS troopers brought in for the grisly job. Each man was offered a blindfold. Each refused. The officer in charge of the firing squad turned and walked away when one prisoner was brought forward. The doomed man was one of his closest friends.

Roehm was not among the unfortunates executed in the courtyard. Hitler could not bring himself to pencil a death mark next to his name. Rather, in what he considered to be a noble gesture, he sent two SS officers to Roehm's cell. They placed a revolver on the cell table and, next to it, a single shell. Roehm was seated on his bunk. He was stripped to the waist. There was no reason for the officers to explain the gun.

It was later reported that Roehm, on seeing the revolver,

shook his head and remarked, "If I'm to die, let Adolf do it himself."

The two officers left the cell. They waited for several minutes in the hall outside, certain that Roehm would finally recognize the inevitable. But there was not the metallic crash of a gunshot. Only silence. At last, they looked at each other, nodded, and unholstered their own revolvers.

Roehm was waiting for them. Perspiring heavily and still bare to the waist, he stood defiantly at the table. The two officers raised their revolvers and fired. There were two shots, so close together that they were almost one. Both bullets struck Roehm in the chest. He fell back against his bunk, moaned "My Fuehrer, my Fuehrer," and died.

Hitler returned to Berlin at midevening. There, he learned that Goering had been working with barbarian efficiency. Just before noon that day, Goebbels had telephoned Goering to inform him that Roehm's capture had been successfully completed. It had been the signal to begin the second half of the purge. Goering immediately unleashed his killers. They struck throughout Germany.

Two men went to the home of former Chancellor von Schleicher. A maid escorted them into the study where the general sat writing. His young wife—after years of bachelorhood, he had married just eighteen months ago—was standing at the fireplace. The men gave Schleicher just time enough to identify himself before drawing pistols from their coats and firing at point-blank range. He slumped back in his chair and his wife ran screaming to him. A shot felled her. The assassins left Schleicher dead and the wife wounded. She died two hours later.

At about the same time, another Goering agent arrived at the home of General Kurt von Bredlow. A friend of Schleicher's, Bredlow was said also to be a part of the Roehm plot. He opened his front door. He was shot dead.

Gregor Strasser, the man who had helped to rebuild the NSDAP after Hitler's release from Landsberg, was arrested and taken to a Berlin jail. He had once opposed some of Hitler's tactics. As he sat in his cell, he looked up to see rifle barrels come thrusting through the small window in the door. Bullets sprayed the room. He dashed about wildly, trying to keep from being hit. At last, he fell wounded. The door opened. A man entered the cell and finished the job.

In Munich, Gustav von Kahr—the leader of the "three vons" who had thwarted the 1923 putsch—was taken from his home and driven to a swampy area outside the city. His body was found several days later. It had been hacked to pieces, most likely by pick-axes.

To this day, no one knows for certain how many people were killed or imprisoned during the "blood purge." Hitler later said that, all told, seventy-seven "traitors" had lost their lives. Of that number, sixty-one had been shot, thirteen had died while "resisting arrest," and three had committed suicide.

A number of the intended victims managed to escape Goering's killers. They fled Germany and later claimed that at least 401 of their countrymen had been slain. Figures released after World War II set the death toll at more than 1,000.

The arrests and the killings were carried out so quietly that the average German was unaware of what was happening. On July 1, Hitler announced to the nation that he had crushed a sprawling and vile plot to overthrow the government; he had tracked down the conspirators and had dealt with them "severely," as all traitors must be dealt with. As had happened before and as would happen again, many Germans accepted his story and many did not, with the latter keeping their outrage and shock to themselves out of cold fear.

Among those who accepted the story at face value was President Paul von Hindenberg. He publicly congratulated Hitler, saying that the Chancellor had "nipped treason in the bud" and had rescued "the German people from great danger."

Hitler's position as Chancellor and his power were once again secure. For once and all, he was rid of a band of real and imagined enemies. But, regardless of von Hindenberg's congratulations, he smarted at the memory of how the President had threatened him with dismissal and martial law. In those threats, the old man had hit him with a hard, cold truth. No matter how powerful the enabling act had made the Chancellor, there would always be a man with a shade more power for so long as Germany had a President.

Something had to be done about *that*.

Legally, of course.

8. NAZI GERMANY

IN 1932, HITLER had told his friends that he could not visualize himself as ever being President of Germany. But now he changed his mind because he knew there was one obvious way to solve the problem of presidential power. On Hindenberg's death, he must take that power for himself. The offices of President and Chancellor must be combined.

It was a move that had an element of danger to it. While the army and navy hadn't yet blocked his way, they might think that now he was going *too* far; that frightening bugaboo of a military uprising loomed large in his imagination. To forestall the possibility of trouble before it ever started, Hitler met with the leaders of the armed forces and candidly told them of what he had in mind. He asked for their support, reminding them of how he had quashed the ambitious Roehm. He then promised that, for as long as he headed the German government, the army and navy would be the country's unchallenged military forces. It is believed that he also promised to expand the army and navy in defiance of the limits set by the Treaty of Versailles.

Whatever he said, Hitler came away with the support he had sought. The military would raise no objections when he combined the offices of President and Chancellor. Now he could do nothing but sit back and wait for the inevitable.

He did not have to wait long. On August 2, 1934, the ravages of old age finally proved too much for President Paul von Hindenberg. He died at nine o'clock in the morning, one month to the day after congratulating Hitler on smashing the Roehm plot. He was in his eighty-seventh year.

While the nation went into mourning for its revered Field Marshal, Hitler moved quickly. At noontime that very day, he announced that he and his cabinet had just formulated a new law. The two leading offices in the land were to be made one and Adolf Hitler was to fill the new post. Further, the title of "President" was to be dropped. From now on, the head of the German state would be known as the "Fuehrer and Reich Chancellor." Finally, the Fuehrer would serve as commander-in-chief of all German armed forces.

Hitler realized that the law was sure to hit many Germans like a thunderbolt. There might be uncomfortable accusations that, despite the enabling act, he was tampering too much with the nation's constitution and acting illegally. To mask this final play for total power in the cloak of legality, he also announced that he did not intend to enact the new law just yet. Rather, he was scheduling a special election for later in the month. At that time, the German people could declare for themselves whether they wished to honor him with the combined positions.

It was, he knew, a gamble and he assigned propaganda chief Goebbels to the task of making sure that it paid off.

In the weeks following Hindenberg's state funeral, Goebbels staged another of his massive campaigns on his Fuehrer's behalf. Oskar von Hindenberg, the Field Marshal's son, proved to be the centerpiece of the campaign. On election eve, he made a nationwide radio address in which he put his father's great prestige to use for Hitler. He announced, first, that his father's last will and testament had just been opened. It contained, he said, "many words of praise" for Hitler.

Then, speaking slowly and somberly, he said, "My father had himself seen in Adolf Hitler his own direct successor as head of the German state . . . I am acting according to my father's intentions when I call on all German men and women to vote for the handing of my father's office to the Fuehrer and Reich Chancellor."

There is no doubt that the speech had a great impact on German voters everywhere. But there also seems little doubt that Oskar was lying in his teeth. The Field Marshal had never liked or respected Hitler. He had named him Chancellor only when faced with no other choice. Why should he then want this "Bavarian upstart" to succeed him?

And there is also little doubt that Oskar was well rewarded for his speech. He was a Colonel in the army at the time he spoke. A few weeks later, he was promoted by Hitler—to the rank of Major General.

Ninety-five percent of the country's registered voters went to the polls in the special election. Ninety percent of their number—a staggering total of 38 million people—voted to make Adolf Hitler their supreme leader, their Fuehrer. Only 4½ million cast "no" votes.

Hitler now took one last step. He had won the support of

the country's military leaders with his promises to them. Now, as commander-in-chief of all German forces, he ordered every officer and enlisted man to sign an oath of allegiance. It was not an oath to Germany but to Hitler himself.

It read: "I swear by God this sacred oath, that I will render unconditional obedience to Adolf Hitler, the Fuehrer of the German Reich and people, supreme commander of the armed forces, and will be ready as a brave soldier to risk my life for this oath."

The long march to complete power was over. Adolf Hitler now stood as the supreme authority in Germany, answerable to no one. And he had made the march via "legal channels"; no one could criticize him or try to arouse any sort of rebellion by saying he was an outlaw who had forcibly grabbed the government. The way was now clear for him to mold his Third Reich into the social and political design that had been forming in his mind over the years.

2.

Before looking at what Hitler did to Germany, two questions need to be answered. They are questions that thoughtful people everywhere have been asking since the 1930s:

Why did the German people and Hitler's political opponents allow him to become so powerful in the first place? And why did they not rise and put a stop to his activities in the next years—years that saw him turn Germany into a police state, years that saw him imprison and annihilate millions of innocent human beings, and years that saw him drive the world into the most savage and devastating war in history?

Why?

Historians have come up with many answers. Not one of

the answers will stand by itself as a complete explanation. They must be viewed together as threads that make up a tapestry of the times and the nature of the German people. Here are some of the ones most often given.

First, the historians point to the political nature of the German people. For centuries, ever since the days of the Holy Roman Empire, they had lived under authoritarian rule. But their experience with a republican form of government had lasted a mere thirteen years. Quite simply, they had not been given the time to accustom themselves to the democratic way of doing things. They were at home with Hitler's authoritarian approach and so found it easy to follow him.

Many historians also point to the respect for authority that seems to be so deeply embedded in the German character. It is a respect that can easily come to see authority as might, and might as right. Hitler was ruthless and vicious, yes. But he was also a strong leader. The German character recognized and appreciated that strength—that authority—and bowed to it.

And, of course, as has been stressed so often in this book, the times must be considered. Germany had been wracked with political and economic upheaval for most of the years between late 1918 and early 1933. She had been thoroughly humiliated in the war and by the terms of the Treaty of Versailles. Hitler, looking so strong and sounding so determined, promised an escape from all the upheaval and humiliation. It was a promise that not only brought millions to him in the first place but that also enabled countless others to accept him passively when he did achieve full power.

Further, as will soon be seen, Hitler did initiate programs that rebuilt Germany's economy. Jobs became plentiful again. There was food on every table again. Germany became a powerful nation once more. All these factors were enough to keep countless Germans from crying out against the brutalities of the state.

Next, there was Hitler's undoubted personal magnetism. His magnificent speaking talents, with their abilities to unleash the emotions of his listeners, drew countless Germans to him. His fanaticism was seen as strength by countless others; even many of those who knew that any fanatic is capable of rash and dangerous acts felt that only a zeal as intense as Hitler's could rebuild a shattered nation.

In addition, there was his personal charm. *Charm* may seem a strange word to apply to a ruthless dictator. But it was there all the same and, thanks to Goebbels' propaganda efforts, the Germans saw it. He came across as a modest though tough man. As a man devoted to children. As a man who loved animals—wasn't he always being photographed with his beloved Blondi, the Alsatian that became his constant companion in the years after the release from Landsberg? And as a man of the people, a man who himself had lived in poverty and who, as a consequence, understood the problems and frustrations of the common man? Carefully concealed was the egotism, the rages, the black depressions, the growing certainty that he alone knew what was right for the country, and—as some of his closest associates had already begun to suspect—the growing insanity.

Finally, there was his old Vienna technique of terror. Roehm's SA had filled his political enemies with fear during his rise. Now the system that he built on becoming Fuehrer was based on terror, the terror of a police state.

It was a terror no longer directed against Hitler's enemies alone. He expanded it to take in the general public and the people close and apparently loyal to him. Four organizations were used to carry it out.

First, of course, there was the SA; though it would never

again challenge the supremacy of the armed forces, this private army bullied the public and ferreted out anyone suspected of being hostile to the Third Reich. Next, there was the SS. Commanded by Heinrich Himmler and with a membership that had grown into the thousands, the SS was no longer simply a bodyguard unit. One of its jobs now was to keep the SA from regaining the tremendous power it had wielded under Roehm. Its other jobs were to seek out enemies within the country and run the horrors known as concentration camps.

Then came the *Geheime Staatpolizei* (secret state police). Created and administered by Goering and known as the Gestapo, its principal functions were to keep an eye on both the SA and SS (everybody was watching everybody else) and to carry out programs of terror against the citizenry. The Gestapo held unrestricted power over the lives of the people. It could make arrests on whim or the slightest of suspicions. It could confiscate personal property without argument. The courts of the nation were not permitted to interfere with its activities or question its outrages.

Finally, there was the *Sicherheidienst* (security service). An arm of the Gestapo and chiefly known by its initials, SD, this organization was a nationwide espionage agency. At one time, it employed more than 100,000 agents to spy on all German citizens and report any questionable activities to the Gestapo. The SD was headed by the sadistic Reinhard Heydrich, who, because of his fondness for executions, was eventually nicknamed "Hangman Heydrich."

In the face of these four organizations, most Germans felt that they had no choice but to bow to Hitler and give him their open support. Those who didn't like what he was doing dared not voice their feelings to anyone. There was no telling who might be a Nazi agent—your closest friend, your fellow employee, your boss, and, yes, even your spouse or child. A wrong word could mean arrest, a beating or torture, and imprisonment in a concentration camp.

The concentration camps, which were collections of rude wooden barracks located in rural areas, sprang into being during the first months of Hitler's Chancellorship when, with the fire decree, he began rounding up so many of his opponents that there was soon no room for them in city jails or SA installations. The first camps were run by Storm Troopers, who quickly began to use them for financial gain. After imprisoning someone, it was common practice for the troopers to demand money of his family for his release. By the close of 1933, there were more than fifty camps sprinkled throughout Germany.

Following the Roehm purge, Hitler took the camps away from the SA and gave them to the SS. Himmler reduced their number by about twenty and enlarged the remainder, organizing them into efficient and brutal prisons. For a few years, the camps housed mostly religious and political prisoners, with the camp populations usually numbering between 20,000 and 30,000 inmates at any given time. Then, in the late 1930s, when Hitler really got down to the job of exterminating the Jewish population, the numbers of prisoners leaped into the millions. By the trainload, Jews of all ages were hauled to the camps where they were starved, beaten, subjected to sadistic medical experiments, and slaughtered.

Once the Nazi conquest of Europe had begun, the concentration camps were joined by a constantly growing number of labor camps. Together, they housed the army of conquered citizens who resisted the invaders or were seized to work as slave laborers.

The largest and most notorious of the concentration camps were located at Dachau near Munich, Buchenwald just outside Weimar, Sachsenhausen near Berlin, and Ravensbruek in Mecklenberg. Ravensbruek was a camp for women. When the countries around Germany fell to the Nazis, camps were established at Aushwitz, Belsec, and Treblinka in Poland, and at Mauthausen near Linz, where Hitler had attended the Realschule.

And so it was that many factors—ranging from the very nature of the German people to their fears of his terror tactics—enabled Hitler to reshape Germany into his own state. The reshaping soon became known throughout the world as the Nazification of Germany.

3.

The process of change, begun on the day Hitler became Fuehrer and Reich Chancellor, continued for the rest of his life, slowing only when World War II began to shatter the country. It was a process that touched all areas of German life. Altered by it was everything from the nation's court and educational systems to its cultural and industrial activities.

The Court System

The German law courts immediately felt the Nazi stranglehold. In the past, court cases had been tried on the basis of laws that had been developed over the centuries. Now those laws were cast aside. Courtroom verdicts came to have one main function: to reflect Hitler's ideas of justice. Hitler proclaimed himself to be the "supreme judge" of the German people. Hermann Goering said bluntly, "Hitler is the law." A Nazi Commissioner of Law was appointed and he warned judges throughout the land, "Say to yourself at every decision you must make: 'How would the Fuehrer decide in my place?' "

As soon as complete power was his, Hitler began weeding

out all judges hostile to his cause and replacing them with sympathetic ones. Next, he established what was known as the "People's Court." Designed as a weapon against Nazi enemies, its job was to try treason cases. Such cases had previously been heard by the German Supreme Court.

Seven judges presided over the People's Court. Of that number, only two were professional judges, with the remainder being chosen from the ranks of the NSDAP, the SS, and the armed forces. The judges heard cases quickly, often giving them no more than a day or two of attention. Defendants were afforded little chance to present witnesses and evidence in their favor. The usual sentence was death. There was no appeal from the court's decision.

A second new court—called the Special Court—came into being. It tried cases for acts that, while not considered treasonable, were branded as political crimes against the Third Reich. Three judges sat on the bench. They were all hand-picked Nazi officials. Defense attorneys were not permitted in the Special Court unless approved by the government. Trials were not by jury.

In addition to establishing the new courts, Hitler gave himself and Goering the right to stop any trial or alter any verdict that failed to please them. Both men abused this power. Once, in a moment of fair-mindedness, the Nazi Minister of Justice decided to try several SS men for their known cruel treatment of concentration camp prisoners; Hitler refused to allow the trial to take place. As for Goering, he once stopped the trial of a wealthy businessman; it was later learned that the defendant paid for Goering's intervention—paid to the tune of 3 million marks.

A special power also went to Rudolf Hess. He reviewed the records of all trials for "crimes against the state." If he felt that the accused had gotten off too lightly, he could take "merciless action" and revise the sentence. "Merciless action" usually meant execution or imprisonment in a concentration camp.

German Culture

All cultural activities—from the fine arts to the daily press—were placed under the control of Propaganda and Cultural Minister Paul Joseph Goebbels. He quickly "Nazified" them all.

Goebbels did so by establishing the Reich Chamber of Culture. It supervised all aspects of the nation's creative life and made certain that everything suited Hitler's personal tastes. The job was accomplished by dividing the Chamber into seven subchambers. Each creative field—the fine arts, literature, the theater, music, the press, radio, and films—was assigned its own subchamber. Each subchamber was in charge of what went on in its field.

For instance, the music subchamber picked the kind of music the German people could hear. Because Hitler disliked modern classical music and thought it decadent, the works of such composers as Paul Hindemith were banned. Likewise banned were the works of Felix Mendelssohn because he was a Jew. The subchamber also sought out the Jewish musicians in the country and saw to it that they lost their jobs.

The subchamber for the fine arts determined which paintings the citizenry could safely see. The theater subchamber reviewed all plays and said which of their number could be produced. The subchamber for the press turned the nation's newspapers and magazines into propaganda outlets for the Nazis; in addition, many newspapers unsympathetic to Hitler in past years, especially those owned by Jews, were forced out of business or taken over by the Nazis; editors were forbidden to marry Jews.

As for the radio and film subchambers, they turned out countless propaganda products; only a few minor foreign films were permitted to be shown in Germany during Hitler's reign. The subchamber for literature approved all new books for publication; it also determined which books could remain on the country's library shelves; and, of course, it banned the works of all Jewish writers.

Long before the subchamber for literature was organized, the Nazi Party had started to rid the country of unwanted and "dangerous" books. On the night of May 10, 1933, a small army of students and SA troopers marched through the streets and entered a square opposite the University of Berlin. There, they set several great bonfires and tossed some 20,000 books into them—books by novelists Thomas Mann and Erich Maria Remarque, by Jewish poet Heinrich Heine, by Jewish psychiatrist Sigmund Freud, and by Jewish scientist Albert Einstein. Into the flames also went the works of such foreign authors as America's Jack London, Great Britain's H. G. Wells, and France's Marcel Proust and Emile Zola.

That night of May 10, 1933, marked the first of the book burnings that shocked and angered the entire civilized world. They were to continue in various parts of the country throughout the Hitler years.

Every German working in a creative activity was required to be a member of the subchamber for his particular field. If he refused to join or was refused admission because he seemed not to be a Hitler supporter, he was no longer permitted to work. The same applied if he was a member whom the subchamber dismissed. Faced with the prospect of unemployment and starvation, countless of Germany's creative people kept their true feelings to themselves and cooperated with the Hitler regime.

But many of the best and most creative minds in Germany fled the country. Among those who built new lives for themselves in such adopted homelands as the United States and Great Britain were novelists Mann and Remarque, and scientist Einstein. Historians have often conjectured how World War II might have ended had Albert Einstein, the "father of the atom bomb," remained in Germany and put his magnificent intellect to use for Hitler.

German Education

Germany's children and young people received a full share of Hitler's attention. His plan here was the essence of simplicity: get to the young with their impressionable minds, stamp their thinking with Nazism, and, by so doing, turn them into lifelong followers. The plan called for the country's educational system to be twisted at all levels to fit the Nazi cause.

To begin, all teachers—from the kindergarten to the university level—were forced to join the National Socialist Teachers' League. The League coached them in Nazi ideas, lectured them on how to pass on those ideas to their students, and made them sign an oath of obedience to Hitler. Then the League watched closely to see that no one strayed from the Nazi path. Unless a teacher was a League member and was licensed by it, he could not find a job. Jews were banned from the teaching profession.

Textbooks and lessons were quickly revised along Nazi lines. Every German student, no matter his age, was taught that he was a member of the master race—the Aryans—and that his people were destined to rule over the inferior races around them. Added was the word that the Jews were the most dangerous of the inferiors; they wanted to win economic control of the world. At the university level, this brand of education was titled "racial science" and was presented in lecture courses. In the lower grades, it was promoted in classroom discussions and games, and in storybooks such as *Der Gifpilz (The Poisonous Mushroom)*. The book contained seventeen stories, all built around the idea that the Jew was a "poisonous mushroom" for civilized people everywhere.

In the elementary and high school grades, the students were permitted—and often encouraged—to taunt and abuse the Jewish youngsters in their midst. At the university level, Jewish students were simply expelled or refused admission.

The Nazi conquest of the young went beyond the classroom. Starting at age six, all boys and girls were required to join the Hitler Youth Movement. It was an extracurricular program with three basic aims. First, it further stamped the youngsters with Nazi ideas. Second, it strengthened them physically with sports activities and a steady diet of weekend camping and hiking trips. Finally, it trained them to be soldiers, teaching them how to drill, handle various weapons, and conduct themselves in battle. The whole idea was to prepare millions of young people to serve as efficient, strong, and dedicated soldiers when, as it must in Hitler's grand design for the future, the time came for Germany to expand her "living space" and settle accounts with the countries that had humiliated her in the war.

At age six, the boys and girls entered an introductory program of sports activities, camping, and Nazi indoctrination. They remained in the program until age ten, at which time they went their separate ways, with the boys advancing to the *Jungvolk* (Young Folk) program, and the girls to the *Jungmaedel* (Young Maidens). There, the children continued their sports and camping programs and their indoctrination work. In addition, the girls received instruction on the role of the woman in the Reich, especially her responsibility to raise healthy children who would be dedicated to Nazism. The boys were made to take an oath of allegiance to Hitler. Similar to the armed forces' oath and taken while the youngsters stood facing a Nazi

A trio of photographs from Hitler's earliest days in politics. At top: Members of the growing DAP marching to a rally. At left: Hitler stands waiting to deliver a speech. At right: he addresses a group of Munich citizens from a party car.

Sporting a flowing mustache, Adolf Hitler is seated at the extreme left in this photograph taken with comrades in World War I. He was known as "Adi" among his fellow soldiers.

(Left) Hitler's mother, Klara. The photograph is undated, but is believed to have been taken while Klara was yet in her teens.

(Right) Hitler as he looked in 1921, two years after taking control of the small DAP group and starting it on its way to becoming the all-powerful Nazi Party.

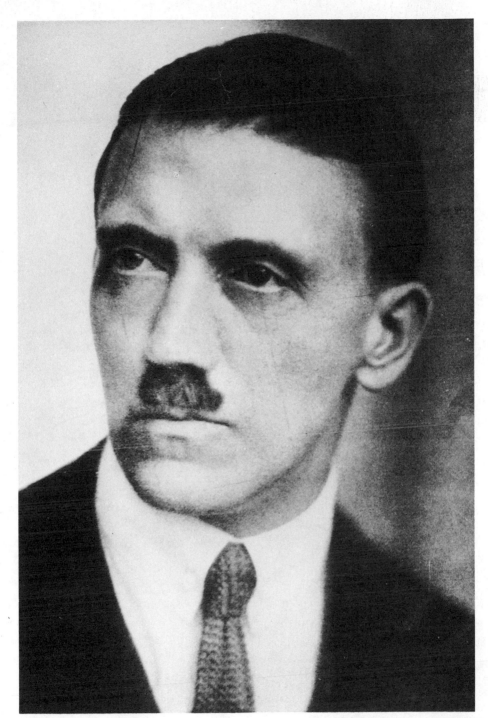

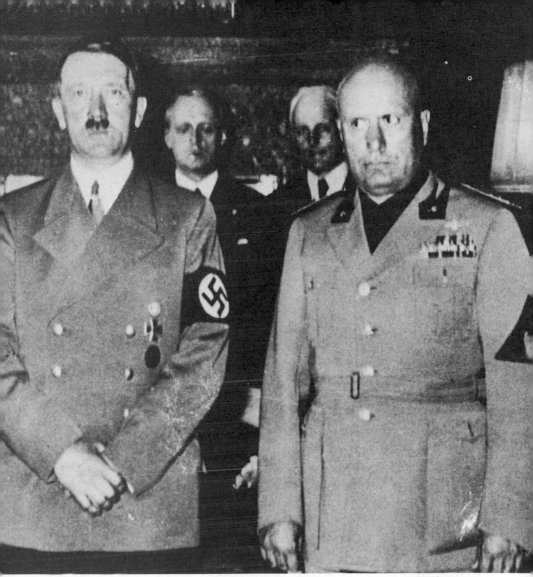

The four men who attended the infamous Munich Conference at the end of September, 1938, and handed Czechoslovakia's Sudetenland to Germany. From the left: British Prime Minister Neville Chamberlain, French Premier Edouard Daladier, Adolf Hitler, and Italian Dictator Benito Mussolini.

(Left) In one of the most widely published photographs ever made of Hitler, he is caught in a gleeful dance step just after France surrendered to Germany in 1940. The picture, with a portion of the forest at Compiègne in the background, is a frame from a motion picture taken by a German cameraman and then made available to the world through British sources.

The stresses of a war that is going against him show in Hitler's face in this 1943 photograph, taken as he listened to a patriotic song at a mass meeting attended by thousands of Germans. With him are Hermann Goering (center) and Paul Joseph Goebbels.

Still dazed, Hitler nurses his injured arm as he walks with Hermann Goering about an hour after the 1944 "July Plot" bomb destroyed his headquarters in East Prussia. At the far left is Field Marshal Wilhelm Keitel. Martin Bormann, who served as the Fuehrer's secretary and deputy leader of the Nazi Party after Rudolf Hess flew to England, is at the far right.

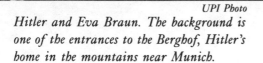

Hitler and Eva Braun. The background is one of the entrances to the Berghof, Hitler's home in the mountains near Munich.

The Fuehrer and Heinrich Himmler

flag, it was a chilling vow. It soon became known as the blood oath:

"In the presence of this blood banner, which represents our Fuehrer, I swear to devote all my energies and my strength to the savior of my country, Adolf Hitler. I am willing and ready to give up my life for him, so help me God."

At age fourteen, everyone moved up another step. The boys entered the Hitler Youth. Here, the activities were the same as before, but now much emphasis was placed on military skills. The boys remained in Hitler Youth until they were eighteen. Then they were either conscripted into the army for several years or sent into the labor service. In the labor service, they spent six months working out in the country, perhaps helping on a farm, perhaps tending to forests, perhaps caring for public parks and roadsides.

As for the girls, their fourteenth birthday saw them assigned to the *Bund Deutscher Maedel* (League of German Maidens). Like the boys, they received military training in addition to their other activities. They remained in the League until reaching age twenty-one. At eighteen, however, many were sent to do a year's work on the nation's farms; during that year, they worked in the fields, attended to barnyard chores, and helped around the house. The young women not assigned to farms were enrolled in the "Household Year for Girls." In this program, the young women spent twelve months helping with the housework in city and suburban homes.

Hitler organized his youth movement while he was yet coming to full power. In 1932, it boasted just over 107,000 members. Six years later, in 1938, its membership stood at around 7½ million. Membership was voluntary during the first years of the Nazi reign, with the fun promised by the sports activities attracting many youngsters. But, in 1939, Hitler decreed that all young Germans must enter the program. Parents who balked at enrolling their children were warned that the youngsters would be taken from them and placed in orphanages or foster homes.

News correspondent William L. Shirer, who was stationed in Germany throughout the 1930s, saw the Hitler Youth Movement at close hand. In his *The Rise and Fall of the Third Reich*, he said that he had to admit one fact. As repellent and sinister as its Nazi teachings were, the program turned out a generation of glowingly healthy young Germans. He found them zestful, filled with enthusiasm, and intensely proud of their country. They were a dynamic young people who would become formidable fighters when World War II erupted.

The German Worker

As was mentioned earlier, Hitler took over Germany's labor unions and installed Nazi officials as their leaders when he became Chancellor. Decreeing strikes to be illegal and ordering employees to obey their bosses and Nazi leaders in all matters, he delighted his wealthy industrialist backers and infuriated many workers.

But the worker fury did not last for long because Hitler quickly set out to rebuild the nation's industry. Jobless men and women went back to work in the thousands as factories began to manufacture all the hardware—all the guns, tanks, ships, airplanes, and munitions—that would be needed to make Germany a great military power again; this buildup not only provided countless jobs but filled great segments of the country with pride because it was in defiance of the terms of the Versailles treaty. At the same time, nonmilitary goods were produced in increasing numbers, providing still more jobs. An example of these increasing numbers can be seen in the automobile industry; in 1932, Germany had been able to turn out a mere 43,000 cars, but the annual total was up to around 150,000 by 1935. Further, Hitler remembered his old love for architecture and launched a nationwide program of building construction; all over Germany, new homes, theaters, offices, and public buildings took shape. He also ordered the construction of a vast network of highways—the autobahn system. Finally, he instituted a number of land reforms that increased Germany's agricultural output.

In the light of all this, it's easy to see why Germany's workers were like the rest of the public is not rising to protest the brutalities of the Nazi state. Though he had taken over their unions and deprived them of many of their rights as workers, they were now better off than they had been in years. There were jobs for all and the hardships of the depression that had brought him to power were beginning to ebb.

Further, regardless of the rights he took away, the Fuehrer was smart enough not to make the German worker a complete slave. Hitler instituted the forty-hour work week so that jobs could be spread among a greater number of people; it gave the German worker more leisure time than he had ever known before. To help him enjoy this new freedom, sports and recreation programs were organized. So were low-cost trips to the seaside, to the mountains, and to foreign countries. The German worker, for instance, could take his family on a week's vacation to the Swiss Alps for the equivalent of $11. Finally, he had the Fuehrer's word that a special low-cost car would soon be available to his and all German working families. It was the Volkswagen—the "people's car."

Religion in Germany

In comparison with his handling of the other facets of German life, Hitler moved slowly against the country's religious institutions. He knew full well that the Germans were, in the main, a deeply religious people. They might stand still for the loss of a free press or a denial of their working rights, but he was quick to realize that an open attack on their faith would kindle widespread discontent and might even ignite a rebellion.

And so, when he came to full power, Hitler presented a friendly face to both the Roman Catholic and Protestant faiths. He told them that they were "essential elements for safeguarding the soul of the German people" and that he wanted "peaceful accord between church and state." The words were followed with what seemed to be a positive action. Hitler signed an agreement, in 1933, with the Vatican, guaranteeing freedom to the Catholic Church in Germany.

But the agreement only seemed to be a positive action. It was, in truth, hardly worth the paper it was written on. Quietly, the Nazi government began to suppress Catholic activity throughout the country. Catholic publications were closed down or made to toe the Nazi line. Catholic schools were gradually outlawed. In time, thousands of priests, nuns, and lay leaders were arrested and sent to the concentration camps; the arrests were always carried out behind the Fuehrer's usual façade of legality, with the Nazis charging the victims with anything from immoral conduct to smuggling.

The Vatican watched the suppression with growing dismay over the years, but was afraid to speak up lest even greater harm be visited on Germany's Catholic population. Finally, in 1937, Pope Pius XI could remain silent no longer. Saying that Hitler had violated the 1933 agreement, he accused the German dictator of secret and then open "hostility to Christ and His Church." On the horizon for Germany, the Pope warned, loomed the "storm clouds of destructive religious warfare."

As for the Protestants, their faith was divided into many different denominations at the time Hitler came to power. Hitler called for them to unite under what he called a "Reich

Church." Most Protestant ministers had no objection to the plan for such a unification. But there were instant objections from many pastors over the man selected by Hitler to head the nationwide church—Ludwig Mueller, a former army chaplain and a fanatical Nazi.

Next, there were objections to the plans that Mueller had for the church—objections to his call that the Old Testament be abandoned, that the New Testament be changed to fit Nazi ideas, and even that the Bible be replaced by *Mein Kampf.* And, of course, there were objections by sensitive ministers—and Catholic priests—to the mistreatment of the Jews.

Leading the outcries was the Reverend Martin Niemoeller, a submarine commander in the war and a man who had once supported the Nazis in the belief that Hitler was the only political figure strong enough to save Germany. Hitler responded by jailing Niemoeller in 1937 for "underhanded attacks against the state" and "abuse of the pulpit." Slapped into prison at the same time were 1,000 of Niemoeller's pastor friends and supporters. Niemoeller ended up in the concentration camp at Dachau; he was finally freed by Allied troops near the end of World War II.

As it was bound to, Niemoeller's arrest struck fear into ministers throughout the country. Beginning in 1938, to keep things from getting worse for themselves and their flocks, the great majority of Protestant clergymen swore an oath of allegiance to Hitler. From that point on, the Nazification of Germany's Protestant churches continued unabated. It was, however, never fully completed and was still going on when World War II ended in the fall of the Third Reich.

Had the Third Reich survived the war, both the Catholic and the Protestant faiths in Germany would have finally been crushed under the Nazi heel. During the war itself, a program for the future of Germany's churches was drawn up. Among other things, it called for the printing of the Bible to cease in Germany; for all crosses, crucifixes, Bibles, and pictures of saints to be removed from churches; for the swastika to replace the Christian cross on church spires; and for *Mein Kampf* to be the only book allowed on the altars of the nation.

The plan was a harsh one. But by far the worst treatment was reserved for the Jewish faith. It was treatment that sickened the world.

9. THE TAPESTRY
OF HORROR

IT MAY SEEM AN ODD thing to say, but Hitler at first moved almost as slowly against the Jews as he did against the Catholics and Protestants. It is true that he took certain early steps, such as barring Jewish students from the universities and arresting many Jews as Communists and, thus, "enemies of the state." But he did not immediately launch a full-scale attack against the Jews, an attack meant to destroy their homes, their places of business, and their synagogues, and meant to slaughter them in the millions. That attack and its attendant horrors were to come later.

All this is not to say that the Jews escaped physical abuse during Hitler's first years. German students, remember, were permitted and often encouraged to harass their Jewish class-mates. When groups of Jewish young people publicly demon-strated against being barred from the universities, club-wielding Storm Troopers savagely attacked them on the pretext of restoring order. Likewise, the SA beat and tortured many of the Jews who were early arrested as Communists. While going about his or her daily business, any Jew was likely to be pushed off the sidewalk or roughly jostled by passing Nazi bullies.

Sickening though these actions were, they amounted to nothing when compared to what was to come. In the main, Hitler's first anti-Semitic moves were economic and social rather than physical. As mentioned earlier, he barred Jews from teaching and from the creative pursuits; as time went on, he also barred them from various other professions and allowed German interests to take over many of their businesses, a move that further pleased his industrialist supporters. On the social front, he enacted laws that kept his "master race Aryans" from defiling themselves by associating with, marrying, or having sexual intercourse with Jews.

As for the physical abuse, it was not only kept pretty much at a minimum (again, in comparison with what was to come) but was also subtly carried out. Jewish prisoners were never publicly mistreated; they were always beaten behind closed doors in SA barracks or concentration camps. Many of the abuses done in public were made to appear to be citizen and SA outbursts over which the government had no control. The Fuehrer, then, was always able to argue that there was, really, little anti-Jewish violence in Germany and that he and the Third Reich were not responsible for what little there happened to be.

Why, after a lifetime of nursing and preaching a violent anti-Semitism, did Hitler now move slowly, even cautiously? There seem to be two basic reasons. First, in his efforts to rebuild Germany's industry, he was beginning to increase her trade with foreign nations. Many of the biggest foreign importers were Jewish. He had no wish to risk their outrage and the loss of their business by instigating a program of outright persecution against their fellow Jews in Germany. As for his anti-Semitic social and economic moves, the importers seemed willing to tolerate them, hoping they were no more than temporary political troubles. Hadn't Jews everywhere, in their long history, faced similar problems and survived them?

Second, Hitler had the wit to realize that many of the world's nations had little respect for him. If their newspapers were to be believed, they were already branding his regime as a brutal and oppressive dictatorship. The avoidance of a wholesale persecution would, despite his social and economic moves, give him a look of respectability in the eyes of the world. With that look, he could lull the community of nations into not taking any troublesome actions against him until the time when his country was too strong for him to care what anyone thought.

In his thinking here, the cold calculation in Hitler's character can be seen once again. He was a violent man, yes; a man of all-consuming ambition, yes; and a man able to fly into blind rages in an instant, yes. But, above all else in the first years of his reign, as he had been ever since the 1923 putsch, he was a man in control of himself when critical issues were at stake. That control, however, was destined to crack in time and then disintegrate. Its shattering would contribute mightily to the catastrophe that finally befell the Third Reich and the world.

For the Jews, the shattering occurred in 1938, when Hitler was forty-nine years old. The events leading up to it involved those segments of the German public who hated the Jews as much as he did. Their impatience with the Fuehrer's caution had grown over the years and now it burst its bonds, with the result that a number of synagogues in such cities as Munich, Nuremberg, and Dortmund were ransacked by mobs and burned. In Berlin's Jewish districts, roving bands of toughs took to painting doors and windows with the word "Jew" and decorating the walls with obscenely captioned cartoons of hanged, beheaded, and maimed Jews. Storm Troopers added to the mayhem by bursting into Jewish shops, destroying merchandise, and beating whomever they encountered. Hitler watched with secret pleasure. These were acts of the people and not the government. The reputation of the Third Reich was safe. Then came November 7.

2.

On that day, a seventeen-year-old Jew named Herschel Grynszpan walked into the German Embassy in Paris. Hidden in his coat was a pistol. Back home in Germany, his father had been severely mistreated by the Nazis, and the boy now intended to take revenge by killing the German ambassador. Instead, he was met in an anteroom by Ernst vom Rath, a young embassy officer. Within moments, vom Rath lay moaning on the floor, his body riddled with bullets. He died forty-eight hours later.

Ironically, in his blind rage, Grynszpan shot a man sympathetic to his problems. Vom Rath had detested Hitler's anti-Semitism and word of his feelings had leaked out some weeks earlier. At the time of his death, his loyalty to the Fuehrer was under investigation by the Gestapo.

The news that vom Rath had been shot and wounded was broadcast to Germany late in the day of November 7. It triggered a fresh wave of anti-Semitic violence. Bands of rowdies attacked the Jewish districts in several cities, looting and damaging their shops. Then came the word that vom Rath had died. It reached Hitler while he was attending a Munich meeting to commemorate the 1923 putsch. He took Goebbels to one side. He told the Propaganda Minister that he knew of the spontaneous outbreaks that had been occurring. If there were further outbreaks, he said, the government was not to discourage them.

Goebbels nodded. He did not take the Fuehrer's words at face value. Rather, he thought that Hitler was telling him to organize an attack against the Jews and to make it look as though it were an outburst of public wrath. Goebbels immediately issued orders to the SA, SS, and SD, instructing them to "organize and execute" a series of "spontaneous demonstrations" on this night of November 9/10.

His general order was followed by specific instructions from Reinhard Heydrich, the chief of the SD. The demonstrators were to make sure that German property was not damaged in the attacks; for instance, he said, synagogues were not to be burned if German-owned buildings stood near enough to be threatened by the flames. Business offices and homes were to be destroyed, but the demonstrators were not to risk public criticism by looting them. As many Jews as the local jails and concentration camps could hold were to be arrested. Special targets for arrest were to be wealthy Jews and Jews in good health.

In the next hours, Germany turned into a living hell for its Jewish population. Jewish districts in cities all across the nation were attacked. Mobs of SA, SS, and SD men, soon joined by the country's rowdiest elements, smashed their way into synagogues, shops, offices, and homes. Furniture and merchandise were chopped into kindling and fires were set. Some Jewish families, trapped inside their homes, died in the flames. Others were knocked to the pavement and beaten as they escaped. Still others—men, women, and children—were shot as they attempted to dash along the streets in search of some safe haven.

The violence lasted throughout the night and the following

day. On the morning of November 11, Hermann Goering received a first written report of the havoc that had been wrought. The report came from the SD's Heydrich. Complete figures were not yet available, Heydrich wrote, but he knew of 815 shops and 117 private homes that had been destroyed or burned. At least 194 synagogues had been attacked. Of that number, 76 had been destroyed.

Heydrich then reported that 36 people had been killed. By coincidence, the number of seriously injured also stood at 36. All the dead and injured, the SD chief added blandly, had been Jews.

The exact death and injury counts for the hours of terror were never accurately established, but they were believed to be many times the number quoted by Heydrich. In the next days, he reported that a grand total of 7,500 Jewish shops had been burned or otherwise destroyed or damaged. The attackers had also committed a number of rapes, a fact that outraged several high Nazi officials. In the main, the rapes were deplored not because they were acts of savage violence but because they broke the Fuehrer's law forbidding sexual intercourse with Jews.

A firm idea of the night's damage began to take shape within a week. In the end, the total damage done was set at about 25 million marks. The breakage of window glass alone amounted to 5 million marks, the equivalent of 1¼ million American dollars. The shattered glass gave the hours of violence a hauntingly poetic name. The night of November 9/10 became known throughout Germany and the world as "Crystal Night."

The violence shocked and sickened the world; newspapers everywhere reported the attacks in detail and accused Germany of starting along the road to barbarity. Inside Germany itself, there was a wave of revulsion among countless decent citizens. Some could not believe what they were hearing. Many had gone to the Jewish districts to see for themselves if the reports of the havoc were at all true. Struck dumb, they had stood at intersections, held back by police, and watched the smoke and the flames. As for the police themselves, they took no part in the attacks but were ordered to be on hand to maintain whatever order was possible. They arrested hundreds of Jews and imprisoned them so that the unfortunates would be safe from further harm.

There was even anger within the Nazi Party itself. Hermann Goering fumed that Crystal Night would damage Germany's business relations with other countries. One of Hitler's cabinet ministers called the whole thing a "mess" and said that it made a man ashamed to be a German. Heinrich Himmler, though his own men participated in the violence, seemed to think the attacks were a poor idea and accused Goebbels of plotting them as a means of satisfying his "craving for power."

Hitler himself insisted that he knew nothing of how Crystal Night had started. There may have been some truth in what he said, for he had told Goebbels only that the government was not to discourage any "spontaneous outbreaks." The propaganda chief had applied his own interpretation to the Fuehrer's words and had taken over from there.

On the other hand, there is evidence that Hitler did know of what was being planned. One Nazi official later claimed that, in the hours just before the attacks were launched, he overheard Goebbels tell Hitler of how things were shaping up. The official said that the Fuehrer "squealed with delight and slapped his thigh in his enthusiasm."

Whatever the case may have been, Hitler certainly approved of Crystal Night. To begin, in the days following, he reacted with fury to the foreign criticism being leveled against Germany. He said that it was proof of how strong "the Jewish world conspiracy" was.

Next, he voiced no objections to an outrageous policy that Goering urged in the wake of the violence. Claiming that the Jews, by their conduct over the years, had brought the disaster down on their own heads, Goering argued that they themselves should be made to pay for the damages that had been inflicted on them. Accordingly, the Third Reich leveled a fine of 1 billion marks against the Jewish population. Further, the insurance money due to Jews for their losses was taken over by the state, with part of it then being returned to the insurance companies. This return was meant to save the insurance carriers. Full payment for all that was lost would have bankrupt many of them.

Whether or not Hitler had actually wanted Goebbels to launch the "spontaneous demonstrations," the events of Crystal Night wrought a great and savage change in him. Gone for once and all was his self-control so far as the Jews were concerned. It was as if the violence in the streets had unleashed so much of the violence in his own being that it could never be penned up again. He now set his Third Reich on a course of wholesale persecution.

3.

Hitler's first aim was, in general, to deprive the German Jews of their property and goods, imprison as many as the concentration camps could hold (letting countless die of the hardships of prison life), and drive or ship as many out of the country as possible.

However, it so happened that, at the very time of Crystal Night, Germany was beginning to expand her "living space" by invading the countries around her, invasions that would lead to World War II. The next years would see German troops spread all across Europe. Among the countries to be entered were Austria, Czechoslovakia, Poland, Russia, France, Holland,

and Belgium. Wherever the German troops went, Hitler's hatred of the Jews went with them. His persecution, then, was extended from the Jews in Germany to the Jews of all Europe.

But there were 9.6 million Jews in Europe. They numbered too many for him to handle. He sent thousands to the concentration camps and made them work as slave laborers for Germany, but it was impossible to imprison the entire Jewish population. And, though he deported thousands to such locales as the island of Madagascar near Africa, it was impossible to banish the entire population.

And so, in the early 1940s, while World War II raged around him, Hitler said that his Nazis must put into effect what he called a "final solution" to the Jewish problem.

By "final solution," the Fuehrer meant just one thing.

Extermination.

The "final solution" became part of the grand scheme for Europe that had taken shape in the minds of Hitler and his party chieftains over the years since the birth of the Third Reich. It was a scheme that envisioned all Europe as a slave market for Germany. For instance, Russia, her culture, and her industry were to be crushed, with her people then to do nothing but provide food for Germany. The same fate was planned for Poland. Half the Slavic peoples in Europe were to be harnessed as slaves for German industry and agriculture; the other half were to be killed. As for Europe's 9.6 million Jews, they were now to be wiped out. To the last child.

In the main, the "final solution" was supervised by seven men. Himmler and Heydrich headed the list. Working with them were Alfred Rosenberg, Julius Streicher, Wilhelm Frick, Hans Frank, and Adolf Eichmann, all longtime and dedicated Nazis. Together, they developed a three-phase program of mass murder that eventually took the lives of 6 million Jews—or two-thirds the total Jewish population in Europe.

The first phase of the program bore the innocuous title, "re-settlement." But there was nothing innocuous about its work-ings. The Nazis would move into a Jewish district and herd the residents aboard trucks, saying that they were to be moved to a new area and "resettled" there. The trucks, however, always ended up out in the country. The prisoners were then marched into great pits and shot. When the ditches were piled high with corpses—and with the yet living—they were filled with lime and covered over.

The actual work of resettlement was carried out by the SS and the *Einsatzgruppen* (Special Action Groups). The German word *Einsatz* means "ready to carry out" and the *Einsatzgruppen* were made up of men—recruited principally from the SA, SS, and army—who would never balk at carrying out any order, no matter the horror that it might involve.

An exact picture of that horror was painted years later when, in the wake of World War II, a number of Nazi leaders and their followers were brought to trial as criminals against hu-manity. One witness, a German engineer who had worked for the army as a civilian, told the court of the "resettlement" he had come upon just outside the village of Dubno in the Russian Ukraine. He said that he saw trucks pull up alongside great mounds of earth behind which the pits were hidden. Then:

". . . The people who had got off the trucks—men, women, and children of all ages—had to undress upon the order of an SS man, who carried a riding or dog whip. They had to put down their clothes in fixed places, sorted according to shoes, top clothing, and underclothing. I saw a heap of shoes of about 800 to 1,000 pairs, great piles of underlinen and clothing.

"Without screaming or weeping these people undressed, stood around in family groups, kissed each other, said farewells, and waited for a sign from another SS man, who stood near the pit, also with a whip in his hand."

The engineer said that he stood watching for fifteen minutes. During that time, he heard no one complain or beg for mercy.

"An old woman with snow-white hair was holding a one-year-old child in her arms and singing to it and tickling it. The child was cooing with delight. The parents were looking on with tears in their eyes. The father was holding the hand of a boy about ten years old and speaking to him softly; the boy was fighting back his tears. The father pointed to the sky, stroked his head, and seemed to explain something to him."

At that moment, the SS man at the pit called for twenty of the prisoners to be counted off. They were told to walk behind the earthen mounds. As one girl passed close to the engineer, she pointed to herself and said, "Twenty-three years old." At the time he had arrived at the scene, the engineer had heard shooting behind the mounds. Now:

"I walked around the mound and found myself confronted by a tremendous grave. People were closely wedged together and lying on top of each other so that only their heads were visible. Nearly all had blood running over their shoulders from their heads. Some were lifting their arms and turning their heads to show that they were still alive. The pit was already two-thirds full. I estimated that it contained about a thousand people. I looked for the man who did the shooting. He was an SS man, who sat at the edge of the narrow end of the pit, his feet dangling into the pit. He had a tommy gun on his knees and was smoking a cigarette.

"The people, completely naked, went down some steps and clamored over the heads of the people lying there to the place to which the SS man directed them. They lay down in front of the dead or wounded people; some caressed those who were still alive and spoke to them in a low voice. Then I heard a series of shots. I looked into the pit and saw that the bodies were twitching or the heads lying already motionless on top

161

of the bodies that lay beneath them. Blood was running from their necks . . .''

In another moment or so, the engineer saw the next group of prisoners walk around the earthen mounds and come to the pit. They lay down on top of their dead and near-dead friends and were promptly shot. The engineer said that the work that day emptied the village of Dubno of its 5,000 Jewish inhabitants.

Though there was only one gunman at Dubno, squads were used in other areas. One *Einsatz* officer wrote that the Jewish prisoners would be assembled and made to give up their valuables, after which they were taken to the pits. There, on undressing, they were marched in groups to the edge of the pits, placed in front of a firing squad, and shot while standing or kneeling. Afterwards, their fellow Jews were made to throw them into the pits.

It is not known exactly how many people died in the "resettlement" program. Though the Jews were its principal victims, it was also used to wipe out Communist officials, foreign aristocrats, and members of anti-Nazi groups. SS officers estimated that more than 1 million victims perished in Russia alone. Adolf Eichmann once set the Russian total at 2 million, but historians believe that he exaggerated the figure to please Hitler.

In one notable instance, "resettlement" did not end in immediate death. A year after German troops invaded Poland in 1939, the Nazis rounded up some 400,000 Jews and herded them into the city of Warsaw's walled ghetto district. There, in an area that could house no more than 160,000 people, they were told to remain, the Nazi hope being that they would starve to death in time.

And starve they did, with some people trying to survive on a bowl of soup a day, but not fast enough to please Himmler. In mid-to-late 1942, on his orders, some 300,000 of the ghetto prisoners were removed and exterminated. Then, in February, 1943, he called for the remaining ghetto prisoners—now just 60,000—to be carted off to death.

But, when the German troops moved their trucks into the ghetto, they ran into a hornet's nest. The 60,000 Jews decided to fight back, using homemade bombs and whatever firearms they could find. Desperate and pushed beyond human endurance, they battled off tanks, rifles, grenades, and machine guns for a month, much to the embarrassment of the Germans. An exasperated Himmler put an end to the situation by ordering that the ghetto be burned down. Rather than surrender and face the brutal punishment that certainly awaited them, many of the Jewish fighters barricaded themselves in the burning buildings and let the flames take them.

The second phase of the extermination program involved the use of what were called "gas vans." These were sealed trucks and buses into which fifteen to twenty-five people were herded at a time on the pretext that they were to be transported to another locality. Once they were inside, the driver started the engine. Pipes led from the vehicle's exhaust to the passenger compartment. The victims died of monoxide poisoning in about fifteen minutes.

The vans came into use after Himmler witnessed a mass resettlement murder and nearly fainted at the sight of the women and children dying. He directed that the vans would be used from then on for attending to women and children. The vehicles, however, were soon abandoned. Killing only a handful of people at a time, they were simply too inefficient for mass slaughter.

Phase three of the program—the use of gas chambers at a number of concentration camps—proved to be the most efficient disposal method of all. The chambers were concrete buildings capable of holding from 200 to 2,000 victims. Once the victims were inside, the doors were shut, hermetically scaling the chambers, and a lethal gas was introduced through pipes. At first, carbon monoxide was used, but it did its work slowly, taking from five to twenty-five minutes to kill. It was replaced by hydrogen cyanide crystals, which reduced the killing time to between three and fifteen minutes. The speed with which death came depended on climatic conditions, the amount of gas used, and the ability of an individual to resist its onslaught.

Gas chambers were installed in about ten concentration camps. The camps, located principally in Germany and Poland, became known as *Vernichtungslager* (extermination camps). Of their number, the largest and most notorious was located near Auschwitz, a small Polish town. It boasted four giant chambers, each capable of holding 2,000 people, and ovens nearby for cremating the bodies of the dead. Estimates hold that about 2 million people died in the Auschwitz chambers.

Most victims of the gas chambers were made to work as slave laborers before being condemned to death. The camp at Auschwitz, for instance, provided the slave labor force for the I. G. Farben chemical works and the Krupp munitions factory. Once any worker proved himself to be too old, too weakened by hunger, or too sick for work, he was sent to the chambers. The same criteria was applied to new arrivals.

The new arrivals at an extermination camp were made to walk past a doctor at the gate. Those whom he considered capable of work were assigned to barracks. The others were lined up for the walk to the chambers. The commandant of the Auschwitz camp later said that all arriving "children of a tender age were invariably" placed with the chamber group. They were too young to be of use.

When the chambers were first used, their victims were told—or quickly guessed—that they had been sentenced to death. Panic and rioting often followed, with husbands and wives clinging desperately to each other, with some people begging for mercy, and with mothers trying to flee and somehow hide their children. To end the problem, the Auschwitz commandant introduced the practice of telling the victims that they were on their way to take a shower. To disguise the grisly truth further, he planted the chamber areas with grass and marked the doorways with signs reading "bathhouse." He even had an orchestra of women prisoners play waltzes and other cheerful tunes while the victims undressed before entering the chambers.

Certainly, some prisoners must have guessed what was coming, but most didn't realize that anything was wrong until they were inside the chamber. There were overhead pipes, but they didn't look like shower heads. Nor were there any bathtubs. And there were so many people being crowded into the place that there would be no space for washing. Then the door—a huge metal thing—slammed shut. The faces of the SS men outside were suddenly pressed against the heavily paned windows, their expressions strangely expectant. And, outside, an SS officer shouted the order to drop the cyanide crystals into the ceiling pipes; at Auschwitz, the order usually came from a sergeant who yelled, "All right! Give them something to chew on." Within moments, deadly fumes were pouring through the room. Now the victims understood what was happening. Choking and trying to get away from the fumes, they fought to reach the door. There, they turned into a frenzied mass, screaming, clawing at each other, smashing at the door with their fists, and at last collapsing into a growing mountain of writhing bodies.

Once the writhing had stopped, the poisonous gas was pumped away and special teams—called the *Sonderkommandos*—were sent in to remove the bodies. The teams were made up of male Jewish prisoners who agreed to perform the grisly task in exchange for food and their lives. Using ropes and hooks, they first pried the tangled bodies apart. Next, they searched each dead mouth for gold fillings that were then knocked out for shipment back to Germany. Finally, they placed the bodies on forklifts or aboard small railway cars for the trip of a few hundred feet to the crematory ovens. After burning, the ashes were dumped in nearby areas, often a river, or (if a report made at the postwar trials was accurate) were sold for the manufacture of fertilizer.

Not only were the victims' gold fillings sent to Germany; their clothing went there as well for further use. Also, when taken from their homes and informed that they were to be "resettled," the Jews were encouraged to bring their valuables to their "new home." On arriving at camp, they were stripped of their jewelry, their watches, their silverware, their money, and their gold spectacle frames. Back to Germany went all this loot, to be placed in bank vaults and credited to the SS. In time, the vaults became so crowded that the booty had to be turned into cash by selling it to pawnshops throughout the country.

4.

There is only one word to describe the extermination program: insane. But quite as insane was the treatment of the prisoners who were not sentenced to the chambers. Along with those Jews capable of working, the concentration camps were filled with people from all the invaded countries—Frenchmen, Poles, Russians, and Czechoslovakians. With callous indifference, the camp officials and guards watched them slave their lives away, growing daily weaker from the lack of decent food and falling prey to the illnesses always to be found in jammed and filthy quarters. It was a grim joke among many prisoners that the lucky died.

Cruelty was to be seen everywhere. The commandant's wife at the Buchenwald camp collected the skins of dead inmates and fashioned them into lampshades; she was soon known as the "Bitch of Buchenwald." In a number of camps, women prisoners were made to work as prostitutes for the guards. The clothing supply in one camp was so meager that the prisoners were forced to go barefoot in the snow. In another, the prisoners once went without water for more than two weeks. In still another—it housed mainly captured French soldiers—the inmates were forced to live in dog kennels for nearly half a year; the kennels measured three feet high by nine feet long by six feet wide; five men slept in each kennel.

How did the camp officials and guards manage to remain so indifferent to such suffering? Obviously, some were sadists who enjoyed thoroughly the misery and pain they were seeing; how else can those expectant SS faces at the gas chamber windows be explained? After the war, one camp official tried to explain the conduct of the others by saying that they were simply following the orders of their superiors. They made themselves not think of what they were doing.

As in the case of the extermination program, there are no accurate figures on the total number of camp inmates who died of starvation, disease, and mistreatment. Some idea, though, can be had by looking at just two statistics. The camp at Mauthausen, a fairly small one, reported 35,318 deaths in the six-year period between early 1939 and mid-1945. In late 1942, Heinrich Himmler received a report that deaths in all camps stood at 70,610 for a six-month period that year. Even without precise total figures, it can safely be assumed that the camp death toll had to be several million.

Adding to all the horror were the medical experiments performed at several camps. Conducted in the name of improving medicine and science, they were actually exercises in torture. It must be said immediately that the entire German medical profession cannot be blamed for them because they were carried out by no more than 200 doctors all told. But, as correspondent William L. Shirer points out, the profession cannot escape the blame of not once speaking up against the atrocities committed by its 200 members. As for the doctors responsible, a review of what they did can leave no doubt of their sadism and insanity.

Many of the experiments were sexual in nature. Countless men and women were sterilized by various methods, with death often resulting. Mechanical and electrical devices were attached to the sex organs of others to see if the damage done would affect future offspring; in one such experiment, a number of teenage girls had shortwaves sent through their sex organs; most of the victims died. In another experiment, doctors attempted to create Siamese twins by sewing Gypsy children together. Again, most of the victims (if not all) died.

A series of experiments was performed, principally at the Dachau camp, to test the survival capabilities of humans, the idea being that the knowledge gained might be of help to the German armed forces. One of these experiments sought to determine the limits of pain and concussion a human could tolerate before losing consciousness or dying. A young boy was led into a room and made to stand in front of a group of researchers. Then he was clubbed on the side of his shaven head until he collapsed, with the doctors noting his reactions in the interim.

A Dr. Sigmund Rascher conducted a number of the survival experiments. In several, he wanted to test how long a man could endure the freezing cold before dying. One such test was later described by the inmate who was forced to work as the doctor's assistant. He recalled that two captured Russian soldiers, both officers, were brought to a large vat filled with freezing water.

". . . Rascher had them stripped and they had to go into the vat naked. Hour after hour went by . . . usually unconsciousness from the cold set in after sixty minutes at the latest," but "the two men in this case still fully responded after two and a half hours. All appeals to Rascher to put them to sleep by injection were fruitless. About the third hour, one of the Russians said to the other, 'Comrade, please tell the officer to shoot us.' The other replied that he expected no mercy from this Fascist dog. The two shook hands with a 'Farewell, Comrade' . . . The test lasted for five hours before death supervened."

At one point in the test, while Rascher was away from the room, a young Polish helper tried to put the two men out of their misery by chloroforming them. But Rascher returned, pointed a gun at his assistants, and threatened to shoot them if they again interfered with the experiment.

In an allied test, Rascher placed a naked inmate on a stretcher out in the open one winter night. The man was then covered with a sheet, after which icy water was poured over him every hour. He remained on the stretcher until morning.

Rascher also conducted a series of tests to study the effects of high altitude on aviators. He got permission for the study when he told Himmler that high-altitude experiments had never before been attempted on humans because of the dangers and the pain involved. The tests consisted of sending inmates into decompression chambers and then slowly withdrawing the oxygen.

In a report to Himmler, the doctor wrote of what happened to a "37-year-old Jew in good general condition" when the oxygen was pumped out until an altitude of 29,400 feet was simulated:

"Respiration continued for 30 minutes. After four minutes, the test person began to perspire and roll his head . . . After five minutes, spasms appeared; between the sixth and tenth minute, respiration increased in frequency." At that point, the subject lost consciousness. "From the eleventh to the thirtieth minute, respiration slowed down to three inhalations per minute, only to cease at the end of that period . . ."

It was a coldly professional report. A far more vivid account of what Rascher's victims endured came years later from another of his reluctant inmate helpers. The assistant said that he had watched through the observation window in a decompression chamber while the prisoners within were subjected to a vacuum that finally ruptured their lungs.

". . . They would go mad and pull out their hair in an effort to relieve the pressure. They would tear their heads and faces with their fingers and nails in an attempt to maim themselves in their madness. They would beat the walls with their hands and head and scream in an effort to relieve pressure on their eardrums. These cases usually ended in the death of the subject."

Rascher subjected about 200 prisoners to the decompression-chamber tests; of that number, about eighty were killed, with the survivors then being executed near the end of the war so that no word of what had been done to them would ever reach the Allied authorities. In other camps, the survival tests called for jaundice and typhus to be injected into prisoners. Other inmates were subjected to mustard gas and poison bullets. Some Gypsy inmates were placed on a diet of salt water to see how long they would live and how they would behave. A number of Russian Jews were killed so that anatomical studies could be made of their heads; the physician in charge ordered that they be put to death in a manner that would not damage their heads; the heads were then cut off and sent to his laboratory.

5.

The savage cruelties seen in the extermination program, the concentration camps, and the medical experiments all prompt a follow-up to a question asked earlier in this book. Earlier, the question was "Why did the German people allow Hitler to reach the heights that he did?" But now, even though they had permitted him to come to power, how could they stand by silently while mass murder was done in their midst? And how could the Jews allow such atrocities to be visited on themselves?

It's one thing to let a man come to political power. It's quite another to let him slaughter people in the millions. Why was not a scream of protest raised?

There have never been any satisfactory answers to the question of why the Jews themselves did not fight back. Perhaps they were simply a people too peaceful, too timid, or too civilized to resist Hitler's attack; if so, the ferocity with which, in the postwar years, they hunted down and disposed of their old Nazi tormentors indicates that they had learned a hard lesson. Perhaps, long-accustomed to prejudice and the abuse that so often accompanies it, they first saw Hitler as just one more passing problem and failed to realize what lay ahead until he had such strength that resistance became impossible. And, in time, resistance did indeed become impossible. The fate that befell the Warsaw ghetto proves the point.

As for the German people themselves, the answers seem to be much as they were before. There was their fear of Hitler's savagery. There was their sense of helplessness in the face of his strength. There was their exaggerated respect for authority. And, if many of them are to be believed, there was the possibility that they did not know what was going on.

As one German has explained, "The concentration camps and the extermination pits were always out in the country. The German people did not know and did not see what went on out there. Everything was done in secrecy. We just didn't know."

Further: "Even the trains that took the Jews and all the others to the camps were moved in secrecy. When a train had to pass through a town, the Nazis would sound the air raid sirens. We'd all take shelter. Then the train would pass through unseen."

On several counts, all this is a pretty hard pill to swallow. First, it's impossible to slaughter several million people so secretly that several million more don't hear about it; surely, somewhere along the line, the camp officials and guards, the *Einsatzgruppen* killers, and the Nazi leaders in Berlin gossiped with friends and relatives of what was going on, and surely the word spread from there. Surely, some railroad worker saw the trainloads of prisoners and talked of what he saw. As for the secrecy of what was done in the concentration camps, it can be negated by the later comment of an officer at Auschwitz.

"We were required to carry out these exterminations in secrecy, but of course the foul and nauseating stench from the continuous burning of bodies permeated the entire area and all the people living in the surrounding communities knew that exterminations were going on at Auschwitz."

And nobody talked?

Perhaps all that can be said is that everyone, Jews and Christian Germans alike, were caught in a contagious madness that was spreading itself over Europe like a Black Plague. They could do nothing but wait until it had run its course in the fever of World War II.

10. TOWARD A NEW WAR

卐

NOT ONCE AFTER coming to power did Hitler ever forget the most basic of all his aims—to make Germany again militarily strong.

From his earliest days as Chancellor—long before he was named Fuehrer—he was determined to overcome those sections in the Treaty of Versailles that prohibited Germany from ever manufacturing military equipment and having more than 100,000 men in uniform. Only with military might, he insisted, could his country ever be respected and feared again. Only with military might could she one day absorb the surrounding countries and thus provide her people with the ample "living space" he had talked of in *Mein Kampf*. And so, between 1933 and 1938, Hitler worked tirelessly to rebuild the nation's armed forces and her storehouse of war materials.

While yet Chancellor, he tried to have the prohibitive terms in the Treaty set aside. At the time, Germany was a member of the League of Nations, the international association that had been formed soon after the Great War; much in the style of today's United Nations, its several dozen member states attempted to maintain world peace under a body of law that ensured equal rights to all nations. In late 1933, Hitler demanded that Germany be put on an equal military footing with all the other members; as things stood now, he argued, his nation wasn't able to defend herself from attack. The League was inclined to agree, but said that military equality couldn't be granted for perhaps another eight years. Furious, Hitler withdrew Germany from the League. It was a clear warning to the world that he didn't intend to be tied down by the Treaty.

But, despite this bold move, Hitler began the military buildup in secret. In defying the Treaty, he had no wish to seem so warlike that France and Great Britain would march in with guns and try to put a stop to his work. Hitler would walk a thin line in the next years, talking and acting tough while always keeping a wary eye out for the dangers of armed opposition. He wanted to grow as strong as possible and take over as much "living space" as he could before having to shoot it out with someone.

Quietly, then, he got down to business. Behind the façade of the Hitler Youth movement, he prepared millions of boys for future service in the army and navy. He had Goering, who would one day command the Luftwaffe (the German Air Force), organize the "League of Air Sports;" masquerading as a string of clubs for young men interested in aviation, the League gave the fighter and bomber pilots of tomorrow their first training. Without fanfare, Germany's factories began to turn out myriad weapons of war—everything from battleships and dive bombers to bullets and hand grenades.

The secrecy lasted for just a short while. In fact, thanks to the espionage of the day, the buildup ranked as an "open secret" right from the start. Hitler soon began to suspect that his old foes, France and Britain, weren't in the mood to interfere with him. They themselves, even after all these years, were still recovering from the horrors of the war and their people had little heart for the fighting that interference might bring.

In 1935, he put his suspicions to the test. He announced that he was instituting conscription—universal military training—in Germany. With it, the country was to build and outfit a peacetime army of half a million men, an army consisting of twelve corps and thirty-six divisions. The announcement completely nullified the Treaty of Versailles. Hitler sat back and waited to see what would happen. As he had expected, there were protests from France and Great Britain and other nations. But they were mild in tone. And there was no talk of armed intervention.

Hitler now knew that he was free to continue the buildup out in the open.

By 1936, he felt ready for yet another test of strength. It was to involve a long and fairly narrow stretch of German territory that ran westward from the Rhine River to the French border. Known as the Rhineland, it was a rich industrial area and had been laced with border fortifications prior to the war. But the Treaty of Versailles had called for those fortifications to be dismembered and for the area to be patrolled by Allied troops. In 1925, the troops had been removed and the Rhineland had been declared a demilitarized zone. Germany was instructed to stay out of the region. If the order was ever ignored, France was to move against her. The French soldiers were to be supported by British forces.

All Germany had smarted at the loss of the Rhineland, and Hitler now decided to risk taking it back. In the dawn hours of March 7, 1936, German soldiers marched across bridges spanning the Rhine River and occupied the territory. At headquarters in Berlin, Hitler's generals held their collective breath. The invading force was a small one—about three battalions— and could be easily and shamefully ousted if France responded by sending in troops. As one of the generals later commented, the French "could have blown us to pieces" had they decided to act. Even Hitler admitted, "If the French had marched into the Rhineland, we would have had to withdraw with our tails between our legs."

But there was no French armed reaction, in great part because France was having political problems of her own and had no desire to worsen them with a border war. Nor did the British threaten the use of troops. In common with a growing number of European statesmen, many British leaders felt that Hitler was justified in retaking the Rhineland. They had come to believe that the terms of the Versailles Treaty had been too harsh on Germany.

And so Hitler scored a magnificent triumph without harm coming to one soldier. Thousands of Rhineland citizens celebrated their return to their own country. Church bells sounded throughout the area. A wave of pride went through all of Germany. A rich industrial region had been reclaimed and the enemies of old had been too frightened to fight back. Hitler had evened the score for one of the insults in the Treaty of Versailles.

The Rhineland triumph was not the Fuehrer's only military action in 1936. Once the area was occupied, he ordered that a new system of concrete fortifications be extended all along its border with France; the system was christened the Siegfried Line. Then he dispatched tanks, airplanes, technicians, and an elite flying unit—the Condor Legion—to Spain.

There, they joined Generalissimo Francisco Franco in his civil war against the first democratic government Spain had ever known. For the Germans, the Spanish adventure was "on-the-job" training for a future war. The Condor Legion practiced for that future conflict by bombing the villages and cities of northern Spain. The fliers destroyed the city of Guernica and virtually wiped out its population. In the end, Franco triumphed; he ruled Spain until his death in 1975.

All the while that he flexed his growing military muscles, Hitler preached peace. Though he knew that his old foes were reluctant to fight, he still wanted to be absolutely certain that he didn't fray their tempers too much. Time and again, in sharp contrast to his actions, he lulled Europe with announcements that he wanted nothing more than to see his Germany strong again and on an equal footing with her fellow nations. In taking the Rhineland, he said, he was only reclaiming territory that was rightfully Germany's; he had no wish to take anything that was not legitimately hers. Representative of all that he said was a statement made soon after he came to power:

"Because of the boundless love and loyalty we feel for our own nationality, we respect the national rights of other peoples, and from the bottoms of our hearts we desire to live with them in peace and friendship."

The actions that were to come in the years following 1936 were to prove him a liar.

2.

The acquisition of power wrought many changes in Hitler the man. Gone were all the meager trappings of his early years—the small apartment, the threadbare wardrobe, the money now and again slipped to him by supporters. Now he wore, and obviously enjoyed, well-tailored business suits and military uniforms. Now he occupied a luxurious apartment above his office in the Chancellery building at Berlin. As often as possible, he went to his beloved mountains outside Munich, taking with him the nation's business. There, he built a sprawling, many-fireplaced villa, which he christened the Berghof, high above the village of Berchtesgaden. The view of the forests and valleys from its great veranda was breathtaking.

Hitler had always been a man of intense opinions, but now his power seemed to make him all the more impressed with himself and his views. He always surrounded himself with friends and staff while at the Berghof, and they were forced to listen to him speak, uninterrupted, for hours at a time on his personal and political views and his plans for the future. The wife of one Nazi official later recalled that the hours spent listening were a "terrible bore." Albert Speer, who served as Germany's chief of war production during World War II, wrote that Hitler's guests, after a day of strolling and sitting about while the Fuehrer talked on and on, were completely exhausted. Speer's comment was made in his book, *Inside the Third Reich*.

On the surface at least, Hitler also seemed to be a different man so far as his relations with women were concerned. He was often seen in the company of some of the greatest German beauties of the day and was rumored to have had many love affairs. To his closest friends, however, most of the rumors were just that—rumors and no more. Underneath, his odd shyness of women in general was still there.

But, despite his shyness, there was a love in Hitler's life. And, despite the rumors of various affairs, the recipient of that love was the principal woman in his life. She was the dark blonde and slender Eva Braun.

Eva Braun, whom a Hitler general once described as "reticent and retiring and a very, very nice person," was the daughter of middle-class Bavarian parents. She and Hitler first met while she was working in a Munich photographic shop. The meeting seems to have taken place about a year or so after Geli Raubel's death, though there are reports that Hitler and Eva became acquainted well before Geli died. Whatever the case may be, Eva's life was soon bound to Hitler's. She remained with him to the very end, at last marrying him in the final days of World War II.

Her life with the Fuehrer was a strange one—strange because Hitler, for some reason never fully explained, kept their romance a secret from the German public; perhaps, jealous as he was, he wanted Eva all to himself; or perhaps he was fearful of the same kind of sensational publicity that the Geli affair had generated. He installed Eva in spacious quarters at the Berghof and saw her only on those occasions when he traveled to Bavaria. She was not permitted to come to Berlin nor was she ever seen in his company at public functions in Bavaria. Only his closest associates knew of her. Between visits, Eva whiled away her time reading novels ("trashy ones," friends said), swimming, hiking, skiing, and watching movies at the Berghof. At times, the strain of her isolated life proved too great for her to bear. Twice—in the Geli tradition—she attempted suicide.

The romance was at least six years old when Hitler embarked on his most daring adventure to date. He set out to realize the dream that the nationalist in him had cherished since his youth—*Anschluss*. He planned to take over Austria and reunite her with Germany. It was a move that was strictly forbidden in the Treaty of Versailles. But the Fuehrer was by now far past caring in the least what the Treaty prohibited.

At first, again not wanting to risk armed interference, Hitler tried political means rather than force to bring Austria back into the fold—and ran into trouble. Austria had been a republic since the end of the war and her leaders weren't interested in the old idea of *Anschluss*; they wanted to remain an independent state, free of everyone, including Germany. Hitler immediately poured money into the Austrian branch of the Nazi Party in an effort to increase its strength so that it could influence a change in this view. In response, the Austrian government outlawed the party and jailed many of its leaders. Exasperated, Hitler summoned the Austrian Prime Minister, Kurt von Schuschnigg, to the Berghof for a day-long conference in mid-February, 1938.

For Schuschnigg, the meeting was a nightmare. Hitler treated him condescendingly and, early on, staged a temper tantrum over Austria's treatment of the Nazi Party. Further, Schuschnigg was a chain smoker and was made all the more uncomfortable by not being permitted to light up in the to-bacco-hating Fuehrer's presence. But worst of all was the written agreement that Hitler wanted him to sign.

It called for the Austrian government to lift its ban on the Nazi Party. Jailed Nazis were to be released. Several Nazis were to be installed in high government posts. Schuschnigg felt himself go weak. These were demands that, if met, would open the way to his country's eventual takeover by the Hitler forces.

At first, the Prime Minister refused to sign the agreement. But Hitler bullied him into doing so by threatening to invade Austria if he did not. Millions of Austrians were good Germans, he raged. They deserved to be more closely tied with Germany.

Once his signature was in place, Schuschnigg returned home. He honored certain of the conditions in the agreement, releasing the jailed Nazis and lifting the ban on the party. But then, in early March, the Prime Minister pulled a surprise. He announced that a special election was to be held. The voters were to be given the chance to say whether or not they wished their country to remain independent. Schuschnigg set the election for March 13.

The move infuriated Hitler. Its intent was clear: if a majority of the Austrian voters said that they wanted to remain independent, the props would be knocked out from under the idea of *Anschluss*. Hitler was left with one option. If he didn't want to risk the election, he'd have to take the country forcibly before the voters went to the polls. He'd have to invade . . .

But that would be a dangerous business. So far, his old foes had seemed in no mood to fight. They hadn't objected to the Rhineland takeover. But that had been the reclaiming of German territory. This would be the invasion of an independent nation. Would it be the move that finally triggered them into action?

Hitler decided to risk the danger. Tanks and troops were rushed to the Austrian border and held in readiness there. All across Germany, Luftwaffe units were put on alert. Then, on March 11, the German forces swept into Austria. They were in Vienna the next day. Nazi Party members and the thousands of Austrians who supported *Anschluss* lined the streets in welcome. Swastikas were soon flying above all public buildings. Austrian Nazis were immediately placed in key government positions.

The takeover was ordered nine months before Crystal Night. But the Jews in Vienna were given a taste of what lay ahead for their kind throughout Europe. SA troops accompanied the arriving German forces. They immediately arrested and jailed 10,000 Jews and looted their homes. Countless Jews were put to the degrading work of cleaning public lavatories and the latrines used by the German soldiers.

Hitler's fears that his old foes might be roused to action did not materialize. There were angry outcries, of course. But, as usual, they were pretty mild. France and Britain were still unwilling to interfere and fight. Many statesmen, among them the British Prime Minister, Neville Chamberlain, spoke out against Hitler's strong-arm tactics. But they agreed that some closer connection between Germany and Austria had always been in the cards. It had been bound to come sooner or later.

In addition, Chamberlain thought that Hitler was once again taking back territory that had been a part of the old German empire. Chamberlain said he was sure that, once the Fuehrer had regained Germany's former territories—first the Rhineland and now Austria—he would be content and would go no further.

He was wrong. With Austria now safe in the fold, Hitler turned his eyes to Czechoslovakia.

Lying north of Austria and east of Germany, Czechoslovakia was a new country, having been formed immediately after the Great War. The peoples of several different nationalities called it home. Among them were a quarter million Germans who lived in the west of the country. It was to this western region—the Sudetenland—that Hitler now looked. The Sudetenland, he announced, had once belonged to the Holy Roman Empire of German States. He demanded that Czechoslovakia return it and its people to Germany. Otherwise . . .

Hitler followed the demand with action. In the summer of 1938, he moved several army divisions up to the Czech border. There were official announcements that the troops were merely on practice maneuvers, but no one doubted that he intended to have them march in and take the Sudetenland if it was not surrendered to him. The Czech leaders, headed by President Eduard Benes, mobilized their army and got ready to fight off the attack.

The cold chill of fear ran through all Europe. For one particular reason, the Czech situation loomed as far more deadly than the Austrian takeover. The reason: some years earlier, Czechoslovakia had entered into a treaty with France and Russia; the agreement pledged the two great powers to come to her aid should she ever be invaded. If Hitler now attacked and if France and Russia lived up to their promise, Europe would be plunged into a general war.

More than ever before, Hitler was risking armed intervention—and armed intervention of the worst sort. It was a clear indication of how his past triumphs had filled him with scorn for the courage of his old enemies.

In September, Britain's Neville Chamberlain stepped into the picture. Twice—on the 15th of the month and again on the 22nd—he flew to Germany for meetings with Hitler. What must be done, the Prime Minister asked, to avoid war? Simple, Hitler replied. Have Czechoslovakia surrender the Sudetenland. Have her do so by October 1. Otherwise, his troops would move in and take the region.

Behind his hard face, Hitler was gleeful. It was good to make such demands of the British Prime Minister. And the fact that Chamberlain had come to him revealed, for all the world to see, just how weak and afraid the British were. Another old score from the war was being settled.

Following each visit, there were frenzied communications between Chamberlain, French President Edouard Daladier, and Czech President Benes. Both Chamberlain and Daladier urged Benes to acquiesce to the Fuehrer's demands, with Daladier saying that France was so eager for peace that she would be unable to honor her pledge to defend the little country. Aghast, Benes turned to Russia. Would she keep *her* part of the treaty bargain? The Russian reply crushed him. Russia pointed out that the terms of the treaty said that she was to help *only* if France did so. Realizing that he had been completely abandoned and knowing that his nation could not possibly fend off the superior German forces, Benes gave in. Hitler could have the Sudetenland.

Chamberlain returned to Germany for a third time on September 28. Two days later, he and Daladier attended a meeting that became known as the Munich Conference. There, they signed an agreement with Hitler that handed him the Sudetenland and cleared the way for German troops to occupy it on his deadline date, October 1. In exchange, the Fuehrer gave his solemn promise to let the rest of Czechoslovakia alone. Hitler's fellow dictator, the strutting Benito Mussolini of Italy, was also on hand for the conference and put his signature to the document.

Europe sighed with relief but with a deep sense of guilt. War had been averted, yes. But at a shameful price—the betrayal of a new and small country.

Hitler was delighted with the agreement. He'd won again. In magnificent fashion. Without firing a shot and without losing a single German soldier, he had claimed another great chunk of territory for Germany. And, though he did not know it, he had saved his own life; several of his top generals had been so appalled at the prospect of a general war—a war that they felt Germany was not yet strong enough to win—that they had begun plotting to overthrow the Fuehrer. The plot died. Six months later, as he had always planned, Hitler violated the Munich agreement and extended his control in Czechoslovakia until the whole country lay beneath his heel.

As for Chamberlain, he returned home to tell cheering British crowds that the Munich Conference had brought "peace with honor." He added, "I believe it is peace in our time."

Ever since, Chamberlain has been often criticized for letting Hitler get away with both the Austrian and Czechoslovakian takeovers. In choosing to talk with rather than fight Hitler, the Prime Minister was following a policy that, at the time, was called "appeasement." The talk, which was carried on in the vain hope that Hitler would soon end his aggressions, has been likened to giving in to a bully. While it is easy to criticize Chamberlain for his policy, most historians have learned not to judge him too harshly.

To begin with, Chamberlain was living in an era when his fellow nations and his own people wanted to avoid war at practically any cost; his actions, though later damned, reflected the prevailing mood in Europe and were applauded by millions at the time. Further, he had little choice but to try to handle Hitler without a fight; Britain had failed to rearm herself since 1918 and was ill-prepared for a war. In talking, Chamberlain was buying the time needed for his country to gird herself for the world conflict that seemed sure to come if Hitler didn't soon change his ways.

Finally, to Chamberlain's credit, he dropped his policy of appeasement as soon as Hitler violated the Munich agreement by extending German control to the rest of Czechoslovakia. The Prime Minister then put all his energies into Britain's rearmament. At the same time, he took a strong step to block Hitler's next advance.

3.

That advance began to take shape in early 1939 when Hitler looked north and east from Germany to Poland.

Peopled mainly by Slavs, Poland had lived uneasily at Germany's side for centuries. In her earliest days, she had been a landlocked country, with German-held territories to the north cutting her off from the Baltic Sea. Poland solved this problem in the Middle Ages by cutting her way northward through those territories and acquiring a wide strip of land (it was more than 200 miles across) that gave her access to the sea. The strip became known as the Polish Corridor because it separated the German province of East Prussia from the rest of the German empire. At the head of the Corridor stood the important seaport city of Danzig.

For the German people, the Corridor was a constant thorn in the side. In the 1800s, the empire regained control of it and held it for more than a century. Then came the Treaty of Versailles. The Treaty returned the Corridor to Poland and established Danzig as a free city. As such, the seaport was to be governed by neither the Germans nor the Poles. But it was clearly under the domination of the latter.

Hitler now demanded that Germany be given access to Danzig through the Corridor; as usual, there was the threat that, were not the demand met, he would march in and forcibly take what he wanted. At the same time, though now thoroughly contemptuous of his old enemies, he made sure that he discouraged them from any ideas of armed intervention should he decide to move on Poland. He did so by signing a treaty of alliance with Italy in May of 1939.

The treaty, which pledged each country to support the other in the event of war, bore the ominous title, the "Pact of Steel." The alliance, Mussolini said, forged Germany and Italy into an "axis of power" in Europe. Because of his statement, the two nations became known as the "Axis Powers" when World War II broke out.

Throughout Hitler's recent conquests, Russia had watched him with growing concern. His move into Czechoslovakia—and now his intended move into Poland—brought the Fuehrer too close to Russia's borders to suit her leader, Joseph Stalin. Stalin now suggested that France, Great Britain, and Russia form an alliance to defend Poland should Hitler strike there. It was an intelligent strategy and, had the alliance been formed, it might well have stopped Hitler for some time to come or for good. A move into Poland would have promised him an impossibly difficult two-front war—a battle with France and Britain in the west, and with Russia in the east. The same two fronts had caused Germany massive problems in the Great War and had contributed much to her eventual defeat.

But the alliance was never formed. Both France and Great

Britain turned Stalin down, France because she was still trying to avoid war at all costs, and Britain because Chamberlain had as little use for Stalin's Communist regime as he did for Hitler and the Nazis. Chamberlain simply wanted nothing to do with Russia. His rejection of the Stalin plan angered many of his critics at home. Winston Churchill, who would soon replace Chamberlain as Prime Minister, stormed that Hitler could not be stopped unless faced with the threat of two fronts. And— if war did break out—he could be most easily beaten if he had to fight on the east and the west.

The pace of events quickened when the alliance failed to take shape:

—Disgusted, Stalin turned to Hitler and protected himself by formulating a nonaggression treaty with the Fuehrer. In signing the pact, Hitler agreed never to violate Russian territory. Stalin agreed not to intervene in Hitler's aggressions.

—Chamberlain announced that Great Britain was pledging herself to defend Poland should Hitler attack. France reluctantly agreed to join in Poland's defense.

—Hitler cast off his last fears about armed interference. He was determined to have Danzig and the Corridor, regardless of whether he triggered total war or not. As he told a British diplomat one day, "I am fifty years old. I prefer war now to when I am fifty-five or sixty."

But Hitler did face a final problem. Though the German people were proud of his conquests, he knew that they shared Europe's horror of a general war. It was a horror that could overcome their past respect for and fear of his authority. He now ordered propaganda chief Goebbels to win their support for the coming Polish invasion and the holocaust that seemed certain to follow.

In a wave of newspaper and radio reports, Goebbels convinced the German public that Poland was the actual aggressor and that Germany was now really acting in "self-defense." The Fuehrer had merely wanted access to the city of Danzig and the Poles had replied by mobilizing their army. That army was now pushing up to the German border. German citizens in Poland were being harassed. German passenger planes had been shot at by Polish guns.

Only one point in the Goebbels reports was true: quite sensibly, Poland had indeed mobilized her army. But everything else was falsehood. The old Vienna technique of the "big lie" was being put to full use. At one point, Goebbels went so far as to have SS men, disguised as Polish soldiers, attack a German radio station near the border. Concentration camp prisoners were drugged and made to look as if they were station employees. They were shot and left to die. Their cries for help went out on the air. Thousands of German listeners were fooled into thinking that they were listening to an actual enemy attack.

And so, by the late summer of 1939, the stage was set for war. The cast was in place, with Germany and her "Pact of Steel" ally, Italy, on one side of the stage, Great Britain and France on the other side, Poland in the middle, and Russia sitting by in the wings. The curtain went up on September 1, almost exactly a year after Hitler had won Czechoslovakia's Sudetenland.

Just before dawn that day, German forces smashed their way into Poland. In London, Neville Chamberlain angrily ordered Hitler to pull back out and gave him until 11:00 A.M. on September 3 to do so. Hitler refused.

At about 12:00 noon on September 3, a pale Chamberlain spoke into a BBC microphone. Millions of British citizens listened as he said:

"I have to tell you now . . . this country is at war with Germany."

11. THE WORLD
ON FIRE

When hitler attacked Poland, he introduced the world to a new kind of fighting—*Blitzkrieg* (lightning war). It was a mobile style of combat that sent fleets of tanks, followed closely by motorized infantry, crashing ahead at dizzying speeds along a series of small fronts. Dive bombers helped to pave the way, as did paratroopers who dropped in behind enemy lines. The Fuehrer and his military staff had been able to develop the new system, which was the complete antithesis of the trench warfare in the first Great War, because of the vast improvements made in the tank and the airplane since 1918.

In the next months, wherever Hitler took it, *Blitzkrieg* was to sweep aside the enemy troops and thoroughly confuse the opposition generals, whose military strategies were still rooted in the past. Even his own generals were astonished at how successful it proved itself to be. They had been certain it would

189

work, but they hadn't expected it to grab up to forty miles of territory per day as it did in Poland.

Poland fell swiftly to *Blitzkrieg*. By September 3—the date on which Great Britain entered the war—the Polish Air Force was a thing of the past. The Polish army, so behind the times that it actually fielded a cavalry unit armed with lances, came to its knees a few days later. The entire country lay in ruins, the result of Luftwaffe bombing attacks on cities, railroad yards, industrial complexes, and military fortifications. The city of Warsaw was the last to go. It stubbornly resisted a brutal attack of several weeks before it, too, submitted to the conquerors.

Toward the end of the campaign, Russia moved her troops into the shattered country and claimed some Polish territory for herself. The move didn't surprise Hitler. He said nothing and let Stalin take the territory as a "reward" for signing the nonaggression pact with Germany.

But Hitler *was* surprised at the British declaration of war, which was followed swiftly by a French declaration (again, as in the first war, the two nations became known as the Allies). Though he had been willing to risk general war, one side of him had felt that, when the chips were finally down, both countries would behave as in the past and would back off and let him have his way. Now he was upset as well as surprised. With their former timidity gone, they would quickly mobilize millions of men, put their war production into high gear, and prove to be terrible foes. His upset was shared by his staff. They knew that Germany was strong, but that, even with her dedicated troops and new style of fighting, she wasn't invincible; no one was. Goering spoke for many when he told a friend, "If we lose this war, then God help us."

In a last-minute effort to avert a fight, Hitler sent peace feelers to Britain and France. Above all else, he claimed, he wanted to see peace in Europe. Both countries ignored him; long ago, he had proved himself a liar. There was only one way to settle matters—and that was in battle. But, before there was time for the showdown, the winter of 1939 closed in over Europe. The war entered a period of calm when not a shot was fired. It was a period that the newspapers of the world quickly tagged with several names—the Phony War, the Twilight War, the Bore War, and the Sitzkrieg.

But the calm was deceiving. There may have been no battles, but there was a frenzy of activity behind the scenes as the nations readied themselves for the bloodshed that would surely come in the spring. France and Britain decided not to invade Germany, electing rather to let Hitler take the initiative and then drive him back. With this strategy in mind, France mobilized her army and reinforced her Maginot Line. The Line was a system of concrete fortifications facing the German border, and it was here that the French high command expected Hitler to attack. The French generals said confidently that the Line was impregnable. As for the British, they shipped a massive force to northern France and instructed the troops to stand by for use when needed.

Hitler spent the time plotting his next moves. The first of those moves was directed against the Scandinavian countries to his north. At the time, Sweden, though not a German ally, was all-important to Hitler's future. Germany did not have iron mines of her own in sufficient number to provide the ore required for his war machine, and Sweden was shipping him vast quantities of the needed material. Because of the ore shipments (and for various political reasons), Sweden would go unmolested by Germany and would remain a neutral country throughout the war. But not her sister nations, Norway and Denmark.

Located on the North Sea, these two countries bordered the route along which the Swedish ore was transported to Germany. Already, the British fleet was beginning to harass the shipments. Hitler realized that, should Britain ever establish bases in either nation, she would be able to throw up a naval blockade and end the flow of ore for once and all. There was only one way to protect the shipments. He himself must have control of the North Sea. That meant that Norway and Denmark must be roped into the German camp.

In April, 1940, Hitler acted. At dawn on the 9th of the month, German naval forces appeared off the coasts of the two countries. Denmark was told to surrender immediately or suffer a vicious bombardment and air attack. The little country, boasting only a meager defense system, had no choice but to comply. German forces moved ashore without a shot being fired.

In Norway, the attack and the demand to surrender came simultaneously. Assault troops poured ashore. Paratroopers were dropped on strategic locations. Bombers hit various cities. The Norwegians resisted the invasion stubbornly, with their leaders replying to the surrender ultimatum with a defiant, "We will not submit voluntarily." But, up against superior forces, they fell before the end of the month. A pro-Nazi government was established at Oslo, the capital city. It was headed by Major Vidkun Quisling, a Norwegian army officer and Hitler friend.

Content that the Swedish shipments could now be protected, Hitler launched his second move. It ended the Twilight War and marked the true beginning of the conflict that would rage for four interminable years. On May 10, 1940, with spring weather spreading over Europe, he threw his tanks and motorized infantry—his *Blitzkrieg*—into Belgium and the Netherlands.

Months ago, the Fuehrer had solemnly pledged never to harm these two small countries that lay to the north of France. Now that promise went the way of so many others. He was on his

192

way to France. Belgium and the Netherlands offered him his easiest route. By taking them, he needn't bother with the Maginot Line just yet. Also, once they were in his grasp, Britain would never be able to sail in and use them as bases for launching an attack on his rear as he proceeded south into France.

The Netherlands fell in five days, with the Luftwaffe, now commanded by Hermann Goering, being principally responsible for the defeat. Bombers poured tons of their deadly cargo on towns and cities. The city of Rotterdam was virtually destroyed. There, 78,000 people lost their homes, thousands suffered injury, and more than 800 were killed. The Dutch royal family was hurried aboard a British destroyer and taken to safety in England.

The Rotterdam attack stands as one of the most shameful acts of the entire war. The bombers swept in overhead while a German officer, riding under a white flag, was leaving the city. He had just spent several hours arranging for local officials to surrender Rotterdam peacefully. The Germans claimed that they were unaware of what he was doing when they ordered the raid. But evidence was produced after the war to show that they knew full well that surrender negotiations were in progress.

France and Great Britain immediately sent troops to the aid of the Belgian forces. For the first time in all his conquests, Hitler ran into heavy resistance. But it proved to be fruitless resistance in the end. Late in the month, the Belgian king, Leopold III, surrendered to Hitler and withdrew his troops from battle. With one opponent out of the way, the Germans were now able to drive the Allies before them and push their way into France.

Once over the French border, the Germans wheeled to the northwest and headed for the English Channel, pushing the Allies ahead of them. The strategy here was to drive the British and French soldiers onto the beaches around the small seaport of Dunkirk so that they would be trapped with their backs to the sea. All went as planned and, in a matter of days, the victims were on the beaches. The German force pressed in on both their flanks, squeezing them into a triangle of land and making escape to the north or south impossible. A massive Allied army was in that trap. The Germans had only to launch a final assault. Then more than half a million enemy soldiers and their equipment would fall into Hitler's hands.

Suddenly, to the astonishment of the watching world, Hitler ordered a delay in the final attack. There seem to have been several reasons for his decision. For one, some of his top generals were afraid that his lead tanks had pushed dangerously far ahead of his infantry; before going ahead, they wanted the infantry to catch up. For another, Hermann Goering got next to Hitler with a suggestion. He advised that the Luftwaffe be allowed to bomb the Allied troops into surrender; a final ground assault then wouldn't be necessary and the lives of countless German soldiers would be spared. Actually, Goering wasn't concerned with saving lives. He was worried that the army was going to take full credit for the Dunkirk victory. He wanted a share of the glory for his Air Force.

And so Hitler's ground forces stood still while he decided how best to handle the final assault. The delay turned out to be his first great mistake in the war. It gave the British just the chance they needed to snatch the Allied troops from the beaches at Dunkirk.

One of the most ambitious and unusual rescue missions in history was immediately launched under the code name "Operation Dynamo." For it, the British assembled some 850 seagoing vessels of every size and description. They ranged from destroyers and patrol boats to fishing smacks, private yachts, and tiny pleasure craft. Beginning May 27, the flotilla moved tirelessly back and forth across the Channel, gathering up British and French soldiers not only from the beaches but also from the wharves of Dunkirk itself and carrying them to England. On May 27, they rescued 7,000 men. Their daily total mounted in leaps. On May 30, they took over 53,000 men out. The next day, they recorded their best score of all—68,000 men.

Just as the rescue operation was beginning, Hitler ordered a final ground and air assault on Dunkirk. But now he ran into trouble. Some 50,000 French troops had been assigned to defend the beaches during Operation Dynamo. They had dug themselves in and they fought savagely to protect their escaping comrades. Also, for several days, the Allies were blessed with foggy weather. It hampered the Luftwaffe's efforts to bomb and strafe the rescue flotilla.

No matter how savagely they fought, the French troops could not hold out indefinitely. Their lines finally collapsed and the Germans poured into Dunkirk on June 4. But the victory was a hollow one. In the days between May 27 and June 3, the ships of Operation Dynamo had taken over 300,000 Britishers and some 60,000 Frenchmen to safety. The men had left tons of equipment behind, but that didn't seem to matter. What counted was that they were battle-hardened fighters whom the Germans would one day have to face again.

Hitler may have delayed in attacking Dunkirk, but he now wasted no time in striking at the heart of France. On June 5, just one day after the seaport fell, 143 German divisions came crashing over the Belgian and German borders. The French army, after sustaining heavy losses in Belgium and at Dunkirk, was no match for the invaders. Nor was the Maginot Line; despite all the claims of its impregnability, it proved to be useless. Moving along a 400-mile-wide front, Hitler's tanks and infantry, supported by waves of Luftwaffe fighters and bombers, hurled themselves south toward Paris. By June 16, the

Germans were in the city and the swastika was flying above the Eiffel Tower.

One day later, the French high command asked for an armistice. Knowing that the country could not help but fall, Hitler had already drawn up his terms for surrender. Now an idea struck and delighted him. The armistice that had ended the first Great War had been signed at Compiègne, a lovely forested area near Paris. And it had been signed in a railway carriage that had since been preserved in a small museum there. Hitler announced that the new armistice would be signed in the same spot and in the same carriage. He was about to take full revenge for the humiliation that his country had suffered on that November morning in 1918.

The Fuehrer, splendidly uniformed and accompanied by a group that included Goering and Hess, arrived at Compiègne toward midafternoon of June 21. German soldiers had already torn the museum building down and had moved the railroad car along its tracks to the exact spot where it had stood in 1918. Proudly, Hitler climbed aboard. He sat down in the chair that had been occupied by the leader of the French delegation years ago. Then he called for today's enemy delegation to be brought in. He gave the Frenchmen little chance to speak. He had one of his generals read the preamble to the peace terms. Then he stalked out, leaving his staff to inform the French of the terms themselves. The shame of 1918 had been avenged.

Correspondent William L. Shirer was standing with newsmen near the railway carriage just before Hitler entered it. Shirer later wrote that Hitler's face was grave but that it was "brimming with revenge." Shirer went on to say that he also sensed a great inner joy in Hitler—an overwhelming joy at the "great reversal in fate" that he had wrought.

The armistice treaty was signed on June 22. Its terms were many. The most basic of their number called for the French

Navy to be demobilized and for France to be divided into two areas. One area would be controlled by the Germans themselves, while the other would be governed by French leaders under the Nazi heel.

On hearing that the armistice pact had been signed, Hitler no doubt could not help but remember what he had written in *Mein Kampf.* At last, after years of struggle, he had brought about the "final reckoning" with the hated enemy who had always wanted to see Germany weak and defenseless. Well, France was on her knees and Germany would never be weak again. For his country, he had conquered more of Europe than any leader since Napoleon. He had made his nation great once more. And he himself had come to a summit of power far beyond any height he had ever dreamed of achieving.

Though he had no way of knowing it, he had also come to the threshold of his first great defeat.

2.

When France collapsed, Hitler felt certain the war was over. Surely, now that she was left alone, Britain would not continue to fight. He told his staff that it was only a matter of days before the island nation sued for peace—on his terms. But he quickly learned that the British people had no such plan. As far as they were concerned, peace with Germany meant nothing but eventual subjugation by Hitler. They were determined to fight on, a point that their new Prime Minister, Winston Churchill, made clear time and again in his eloquent speeches.

The British stubbornness infuriated Hitler, as did Churchill's contempt for him; whenever the Prime Minister mentioned Hitler's name, he insisted on calling him "Corporal Hitler," literally spitting out the words as he spoke. All right. If Britain would not recognize the inevitable, then she must have the fight she was asking for. In July, 1940, Hitler ordered his generals to prepare for "Operation Sea Lion," the invasion of the island from the sea. It was an order that the generals didn't like at all. A sea invasion promised to be a disaster. For one thing, their troops had little experience in assault landings. For another, the British Navy and the Royal Air Force (RAF), already patrolling the English Channel in the expectation of trouble, were sure to raise havoc with the transports carrying the invasion force.

Before Sea Lion could be launched, the generals said, Goering's Luftwaffe would have to get the British Navy out of the way. Goering replied that he would not only cripple the Navy but would also bomb the RAF out of existence. After all, he had 3,000 planes to Britain's 800. Hitler told him to make good on his boast.

The Luftwaffe began its attacks in August, starting with British shipping and ports, and then adding industrial sites to its list of targets. Within a few days, it put the emphasis on the RAF bases that were sprinkled throughout the country. The bases took a severe pounding, but, in all, the strikes did not turn out as well as Goering had anticipated. The British were equipped with a new weapon—radar—and it took away the element of surprise. Pinpointing the exact locations of incoming bombers as it did, it enabled the RAF often to intercept them before they reached their targets. Further, the RAF pilots proved themselves to be superb fighters. For every one of their losses, they sent two German planes down in flames.

Hitler and Goering thought the problem could be easily solved. They simply struck with a greater number of planes in the knowledge that the RAF didn't have enough defenders to stop them all. For each strike, the Germans now put between 500 and 1,000 planes in the air.

In justice to Hitler and Goering, it must be said that the

initial raids were, in the main, limited to legitimate military targets—shipping, industrial sites, and air bases. On August 24, however, a navigational error caused several Luftwaffe fliers to drop their bombs on homes in the city of London. The British, thinking the London mishap to be deliberate, ordered a retaliatory strike and, on the following day, Berlin suffered its first air raid of the war. The raid was a minor one, carried out by just a few bombers, and little physical damage was done. But it sent a shock wave throughout Germany. The Fuehrer had always promised the people that their cities would be safe. Well, he'd been mistaken! Germany's confidence in its until-now invincible leader was badly shaken.

Enraged and embarrassed, Hitler suddenly changed his tactics. Ever since increasing the size of his striking forces, he had been doing serious damage and was actually on the brink of crippling the RAF. Now, to avenge the Berlin raid, the Fuehrer cancelled the RAF targets and called for an all-out attack— an air *Blitzkrieg*—on London. He was also sure the attack would net him more than revenge. There was every chance—so he thought—that the destruction of their capital city would bring the British to their senses. They would at last ask for peace and render the dangerous Operation Sea Lion unnecessary.

He was wrong. His mistake here proved to be a far greater blunder than the one at Dunkirk.

The London strikes began in September. They continued for fifty-seven days—first in the daylight and then at night— inflicting heavy business and residential damage, killing and injuring thousands, and leaving thousands more homeless. But the Germans also suffered heavily. Some 400 Luftwaffe aircraft participated in the first strike; more than one-quarter of their number were brought down. Further—and here Hitler's mistake was most clearly seen—the RAF quickly strengthened itself now that its bases were safe and went out to meet the attackers.

The incoming bombers were no match for the highly maneuverable fighters, especially the deadly Spitfires. The defending pilots brought down scores of enemy planes.

Hitler had planned to launch Operation Sea Lion sometime in late 1940. But, unable to break the back of the RAF (thanks, again, to his precipitate change of tactics), he had to keep postponing the invasion. At last, Hitler called it off for the winter of 1940–41; he never took it up again, but turned to other campaigns. The air attacks were also suspended temporarily. When they commenced again, they were carried out on a much reduced scale and, though they continued for two years or more, they were to trouble Britain only intermittently.

What the newspapers of the world had been calling "The Battle of Britain" came to an end with the cessation of the air attacks. The clear victors were the British. Their country was still in the war and would become the base for the several million troops that would assault Hitler's Europe in just a few years. The Luftwaffe had suffered wounds from which it would never fully recover; it would never again be master of the skies over Europe. The war, after beginning so gloriously for Hitler, was now turning against him.

He was at the start of the long road that would lead to Germany's destruction and his death.

3.

Unable to invade and conquer Britain, Hitler in late 1940 decided to strike at her from another quarter. First, he invaded Greece and Yugoslavia, where the British maintained important military bases. Then, accompanied by his ally, Italy (Mussolini had entered the war on June 10 so that he could grab a share of collapsing France), he threw troops into North Africa. His aim here was to choke off Britain's supply of oil by taking the Suez Canal, the waterway along which oil was transported from the Middle East.

At first, the North African campaign went well, with General Erwin Rommel's *Panzer* (tank) divisions driving back the British troops. But, once again, Hitler added to the list of his mistakes. When his generals advised that he commit a major share of the German army to Africa so that the Canal could be quickly won, he refused. He had other ideas for 3 million of his soldiers. They were to be used in an invasion of Russia. As a result, his African forces were never able to take the Canal and were finally defeated in 1943.

Hitler's decision to attack Russia despite the nonaggression pact with Stalin was based on several factors. For one, Stalin himself had recently violated the pact by invading several small nations close to the Fuehrer's holdings. One of the victims was Rumania, which lay on the Polish and Czech borders. It was a vital source of oil and food for Germany. The moves convinced Hitler that Stalin was getting ready to take sides with the stubborn British.

The overriding factors, however, were two—his long-standing hatred of communism, plus the idea of *Lebensraum* that he had voiced in *Mein Kampf.* The finest "living space" for an expanding Germany, remember, was to be found in Russia. The time, then, had come to take that space, put an end to Stalin's conquests, and smash Russian communism.

Under the code name "Operation Barbarossa," the Russian campaign was planned in late 1940 and early 1941. Then, coming mainly through Poland, some 120 divisions swept over the Russian frontier on June 22, 1941. Attacking along a front of several hundred miles, they fanned out in three directions— east toward Moscow, north toward the city of Leningrad, and south toward the city of Rostov and the rich lands beyond it.

The attack caught the Russians by surprise. At first, their

troops fell back in confusion and sustained heavy losses. But then—an ill omen for the Hitler venture—their retreat became an orderly one. As they fell back, they were waiting for the right moment to counterattack. That moment came when the always-severe Russian winter closed down around the invaders. The German tanks and trucks became mired in the mud and then the snow. The troops were bone weary from fighting, and they were neither adequately uniformed for the bitter cold nor accustomed to it; thousands of soldiers began to fall victim to frostbite. Finally, they were now so deep into Russia—some units were right at the gates of Moscow itself—that the problem of getting supplies to them from home had turned into a nightmare.

On December 6, the Russians launched their counteroffensive. General Georgi Zhukov threw more than 100 divisions, all properly clothed and all accustomed to the weather, at the exhausted invaders. At Berlin, a pale Hitler listened to the incoming reports. For the first time in his career, he was hearing that his troops were in retreat—at both Moscow in the north and Rostov in the south.

Hitler's generals advised that he evacuate the troops from Russia before the winter and Zhukov completely destroyed them. The Fuehrer answered with a shriek: the troops must stay where they were, falling back as little as possible. The master race must not cut and run! His stubbornness resulted in an appalling sacrifice of life. The counterattack raged through the winter, finally ending in March, 1942. By that time, 1 million of the 3 million men whom Hitler had committed to the invasion had been lost. Of that number, over 200,000 were dead, and 720,000 wounded. About 112,000 had been knocked out with frostbite. Some 48,000 were listed as missing.

Yet, despite the terrible losses, the Hitler forces were still deep in Russian territory. As ordered, they had held on. Now he put them on the offensive again. The future was to hold further horrors for them.

As if the Russian beating weren't enough, Hitler now found himself facing a new enemy—the United States.

The United States had managed to remain neutral since 1939, though she had supplied Britain with war materials all during that time. But on December 7, 1941, the day after Zhukov unleashed his counteroffensive, the Japanese attacked the American naval base at Pearl Harbor in Hawaii, at the same time hitting the British in the Indo-China area. Both the United States and Great Britain declared war on Japan. Hitler had long held a mutual defense treaty with Japan, a country that, as he was doing in Europe, was following an expansionist treaty in the Pacific. He immediately declared war on the U.S. The American response was a declaration of war against the Axis powers.

Hitler's generals were appalled at the turn of events; along with Britain and Russia, another major industrial power was now pitted against them; the terrible history of World War I was beginning to repeat itself. But the Fuehrer didn't share their fears. First, he looked on the United States as a weakling nation because she had not gone to war months ago when his submarines had begun sinking her merchant ships bound for Great Britain with military cargoes. Second, he felt certain that he would never have to battle the Americans. They would be kept too busy with the Japanese.

Two more horrendous mistakes.

4.

Ever since entering politics, Hitler had been blessed with a spectacular amount of energy. He was capable of working long hours each day. His usual day began at dawn—with a breakfast of rolls and fruit juice or milk—and extended well into the evening; a few moments were taken in the afternoon for a stroll through the gardens behind the Chancellery building. On finally leaving his office at night, the Fuehrer would have friends and staff come upstairs to his apartment for a private showing of a movie, after which, still too keyed-up for sleep, he would sit and talk for a time. When not at his Berlin desk, Hitler was to be found at his various field headquarters, directing the war from there. Whenever possible, he fitted in trips to the Berghof for visits with Eva Braun.

No matter how busy he was, his old interest in art and architecture always won a goodly share of his time, prompting some friends to joke that he was, at heart, still an artist rather than a politician. In 1933, while yet struggling to win full power in Germany, he had devoted much attention to the construction of a magnificent art museum in Munich. Now, at the height of the war, countless hours were spent on plans to turn Berlin into the queen city of Europe once the fighting had ended. While his generals cooled their heels in his outer office, the Fuehrer pored over architectural drawings or stood admiring the models that he had ordered made of the massive public buildings of the future.

But the strains of the war were great and, regardless of his energy, Hitler was a middle-aged man and they were beginning to leave their marks on him. By the time of the Russian disaster, his face had become deeply lined. His eyes were puffed with fatigue. There was gray showing in his hair. And his careful self-control of the past was disintegrating. More and more, his volatile temper was taking over, throwing him into blind rages whenever his generals brought him bad news. More and more, he was blaming them for all that was going wrong. More and more, he was refusing to heed their counsel and screaming that he alone knew best how to conduct the war.

There were also other ways in which the strains were showing themselves. They worried the people around Hitler quite as much as his diminishing self-control. For one, the Fuehrer had long been interested in astrology, but it now seemed to be developing into an obsession. He depended much on the advice of several astrologers and showed an alarming reluctance to act unless their predictions were favorable ones. As some of his most hard-headed generals put it, astrology might be an entertaining hobby but it had no place in the running of a government and a war.

(Hitler, incidentally, was not alone in his belief in astrology. It was shared by Heinrich Himmler and Rudolf Hess, not to mention a number of lesser Nazi lights who found it politically wise to express an interest in the stars. In fact, one of the most fantastic episodes of the war had to do with astrology. In May, 1941, Hess climbed into a fighter plane and, leaving behind a garbled note for Hitler, flew to Scotland. He surrendered himself to the British authorities and said that, on his own, he had come to arrange a peace treaty. Among the reasons that he later gave for his flight was the fact that his astrologer had just told him he was destined to bring peace to Europe. Hess spent the rest of the war in prison.)

On top of all else, Hitler's closest associates were worried about the health care being given him by his personal physician, Dr. Theodor Morell. They looked on Morell as a quack—and with good reason. He was a sloppily dressed man who seemed totally unconcerned about his personal cleanliness. He often worked with dirty hands and fingernails. He was known to use the same hypodermic needle on two patients without bothering to sterilize it. There was even a story that he had once wiped a table with a bandage and then wrapped an injured arm with it.

Morell had been Hitler's personal doctor since the mid-1930s when he cured a skin problem that had bothered the Fuehrer for some time and had frustrated several other physicians. From then on, Morell had treated Hitler's various physical ills (they ranged from a chronic gastric problem to a gradual hardening of the arteries) and his recurring depressions with injections and pills. The exact medications used in many of them remain unknown, but it is thought that some injections contained vitamins and stimulants to enliven the Fuehrer when events so demanded, while the pills contained tranquilizers to relax and quiet him. It was rumored that the pills contained anything from strong tranquilizing agents to morphine.

Hitler's friends believed that, over the years, Morell gave the Fuehrer more than 1,000 injections. Goering had a nickname for the doctor: "The Master of the Imperial Needle." The use of the injections and the pills increased steadily as the passing years brought Hitler a mounting number of setbacks and problems.

To many of the people around the Fuehrer, all that they were seeing seemed to point in just one direction. Hitler's health was growing more precarious as the weight of the war pressed down on him. And, worse, his sanity—always a question mark in the minds of many of his closest associates—was collapsing. Among themselves, they began to face the fact that Germany was in the hands of a madman and that he was taking her down to disaster.

He was. From the Battle of Britain and the Russian invasion onward, each year brought terrible setbacks.

In February, 1943, Germany suffered its worst defeat to date. German troops had been about to take the city of Stalingrad in southern Russia when Hitler, over the objections of his generals, cut away some of the soldiers so that they could attempt the capture of nearby oil fields. A massive Russian force, again using the bitter winter as an ally, attacked the troops that were left behind. Some 285,000 Germans were slaughtered. The remainder—91,000 exhausted and frostbitten men—were easily taken prisoner.

Barely three months later, the war in North Africa came to an inglorious end. More than a quarter-million German soldiers surrendered to British and American troops. The United States had joined the North African fighting in 1942 and had shown Hitler the mistake of thinking that this "weakling nation" would be too busy with the Japanese ever to face him. With millions of men at its disposal, the U.S. was proving itself capable of waging a multifront war.

Then, in July, the British and the Americans began to stab at Germany's underbelly by landing in Sicily and then Italy. Mussolini's government fell on July 24 and the dictator fled; later, he and his mistress were tracked down by his Italian enemies and executed. Italy dropped out of the war in September, leaving Germany alone.

But the worst blow came in 1944. Ever since entering the war, the United States had been sending masses of troops to Britain, there to join soldiers from all the countries of the British Commonwealth, as well as fighters who had escaped from the occupied European nations. It was clear that an all-out attack on Hitler's "Fortress Europe" was in the making.

It came on June 6, 1944, when the first wave of British and American troops—five divisions in all—were transported across the English Channel to the French coast. Once they had secured a beachhead at Normandy, they were followed by millions of troops. The Allied armies, with General Dwight D. Eisenhower of the United States serving as Supreme Commander and General Bernard Law Montgomery of Britain commanding the ground forces, speared deep into France and headed for Germany.

Once the invasion of Europe had begun, Hitler's generals

knew that the war was over. Their country would soon be overrun by massive forces. Worse, those massive forces were now coming from two directions because the Russians, after defending their country for three years, were also on the move. Pushing the German troops ahead of them, they were thrusting in from the east.

But, whenever they expressed their opinions to Hitler, the generals ran into a stone wall of rage. He stormed that Germany would never give up and that they were cowards for even thinking of surrender. In some way, he would find an ultimate victory. So great was his frenzy that one officer said—privately, of course—that he was behaving like a "rat caught in a trap." To a growing number of officers, there seemed only one way to save Germany. The "cornered rat" must be killed.

Out of that realization came what was known as the "July Plot." Developed by a small group of high-ranking officers, it was carried out by Colonel Klaus von Stauffenberg, a much-decorated soldier and member of an old noble family. On July 20, 1944, he joined a staff meeting that Hitler was conducting at army headquarters in East Prussia. He held a briefcase; it contained a time bomb. Stauffenberg placed the case under the conference table and, as the Fuehrer was discussing his Russian problems with the surrounding officers, he quietly left the room. Moments later, the room was torn apart by an explosion.

Dust and smoke filled the place and poured out through the entrance. A figure appeared in the doorway and turned into a blackened and staggering Hitler. His uniform was torn and his right arm, temporarily paralyzed, hung uselessly at his side. He was burned and shaken. But he was alive. By miracle, it seemed.

It was later learned that an officer at the meeting was responsible for the miracle. After Stauffenberg had departed, the man had accidentally kicked the case away from Hitler and had thus saved his life. Every officer in the room suffered burns to one degree or another. Several had been killed.

If there had been any lingering doubts about Hitler's growing madness, they were dispelled. Literally frothing at the mouth, he told his staff that his survival had been a sign from God that he was destined to lead Germany to victory. He yelled instructions to Goering and Himmler: they were to track down anyone even remotely connected with the plot. As a result, an astonishing number of German officials and military officers of virtually every rank—about 7,000 in all—were arrested and executed. Piano wire rather than rope was used in the executions, so that the victims, their eyes bulging and their faces purpling, were made to die slowly of strangulation. General Erwin Rommel, whose *Panzer* divisions had performed so magnificently in North Africa, was among the suspected officers. Because of his prestige, he was given the choice to kill himself or see his family imprisoned. He took poison.

Stubbornly and fiercely, all through the remaining months of 1944, Hitler clung to the belief that he would bring Germany to final victory. He unveiled a new weapon—a "pilotless plane," a rocket—that he threw at Britain in an effort to demoralize her people and that they quickly christened "the buzz bomb." In December of the year, with the Allied troops now close to the German border and pouring into Belgium, he launched a desperate counterattack. He threw a mere twenty-one divisions against a force numbering in the millions. The "Battle of the Bulge," as the Allied soldiers called it, raged for a few weeks in the snows of Belgium before the Germans were flung back.

By early 1945, the Allies were flooding across the Rhine and into Germany. Russian troops were pressing in from the opposite direction. The British and American air forces—the one operating in daylight and the other at night—were pounding

German cities, chief among them Berlin itself, and reducing them to twisted rubble.

The end was in sight.

5.

On January 16, 1945, Hitler entered the underground bunker that was to be his final home. Berlin was now being so heavily bombed that further work in his Chancellery office was impossible.

Entered from the Chancellery building, the bunker lay fifty feet below ground and was spread out beneath the Chancellery gardens. It was a network of concrete-walled corridors, offices, conference rooms, and kitchen, dining, and recreational areas, all painted a dull gray. Three rooms—a study, a bedroom, and a living room—were reserved for Hitler. The bedroom, which was furnished with a single bed, a nightstand, and a dresser, measured about ten feet wide by fifteen feet long. It was hardly any larger than his first bedroom apartment in Munich.

It was here—surrounded by army officers, SS guards, Chancellery secretaries, and his personal staff—that Hitler was to spend the final 105 days of his life. Of the oldest of his Nazi associates, only Goebbels came down into the bunker, bringing Frau Goebbels and their six children with him. Goering and Himmler were elsewhere in Germany and were locked in a power struggle over who would succeed the Fuehrer when the country fell, as surely it must, in the next few weeks.

Throughout the bunker stay, that power struggle infuriated Hitler, especially when a report reached him that Himmler had attempted to contact the Allied powers and negotiate a separate peace with them. Hitler finally dismissed both men from the Nazi Party and stripped them of their jobs. Two friendships that dated back to the very beginnings of the party had ended. He must have felt very alone.

By now, his mind was almost assuredly gone. He kept insisting that somehow he would find a way to victory. It was a delusion to which the devoutly loyal Goebbels catered. On one occasion, he came to Hitler with the word that an astrologer had said that the stars were now most propitiously situated for the Fuehrer. Hitler nodded wildly. He would be great again! He was certain of it! At that moment, the Russians, who had charged over the German border some weeks earlier, were actually penetrating the outskirts of Berlin.

In his lucid moments, Hitler made plans to leave Berlin by April 20 at the latest. He would go to his beloved Berghof and direct the final phases of the war from there. The plan never came to pass. The Allied troops coming in from the west cut off his avenue of air escape long before the departure date.

But the lucid moments were pitifully few. At all other times, his thinking seemed to be that of a lunatic. On one occasion, screaming at his generals for bringing the news of the latest Allied advances, he demanded that all Germans pack up and move to the center of the country, there to defend the nation to the last man; the order was never carried out. On another occasion, he sent troops of Hitler Youth—boys of no more than fifteen or sixteen—to defend the Berlin streets against the oncoming Soviet tanks. That order *wasn't* cancelled.

The life around him in the bunker seemed as mad as he. Each night, after he had retired to his little bedroom, there were parties, with the revelers laughing uproariously and dancing to phonograph records in a desperate attempt to forget the horror that was closing in around them. Capsules containing poison were passed out among the bunker personnel, to be used by those who couldn't tolerate the thought of falling into Soviet hands. The women secretaries were terrified of what would happen to them when the first Russian soldiers entered the bunker; between air raids each day, they carried pistols up to a nearby park and practiced target shooting.

Eva Braun, tall and splendidly dressed, came to the bunker in mid-April to be at Hitler's side during these final days. She found a broken man. His face was now a pasty color. His voice was hoarse, sometimes little more than a whisper. On occasion, he was so ill and so depressed that he would take to his bed for hours at a time. He walked with a shambling gait and his hands trembled violently whenever he tried to pick up anything. A doctor at the scene suspected that Hitler was suffering from Parkinson's disease. More than likely, he was also suffering from Dr. Morell's various medications.

The Morell injections containing stimulants were now being given almost daily. In fact, whenever bad news of the war threatened to crush Hitler, he immediately called for the doctor and his syringe. And Morell had recently prescribed some charcoal-colored pills—the bunker people called them "the black pills"—for Hitler's chronic and painful gastric problem. Two to four were to be taken at each meal. Morell, with his usual professional laxity, didn't bother to learn their ingredients. When another physician—the respected Dr. Erwin Giesing of Berlin—checked them, he was stunned to find that they contained strychnine and atropine, both lethal drugs if not correctly prescribed and carefully administered.

Giesing and several others suspected that Morell might be deliberately trying to poison the Fuehrer. But Morell pleaded his innocence (indications are that he actually was innocent) and Hitler at first believed him. In a matter of days, though, Hitler grew suspicious of the man and ordered him to leave the bunker. Morell never got over the hurt and humiliation of his dismissal. He died soon after the war.

Though the bunker secretaries went outside almost daily for their target practice, Hitler rarely sought the fresh air. Clinging savagely to the hope of a miracle victory, watching the collapse of his Third Reich, and daily receiving visitors with dread news of the latest Allied victories, he worked almost round-the-clock in his suite of rooms, going to bed just before dawn and arising by nine or ten in the morning. Occasionally, when things were quiet at night, he would walk with his dog in what was left of the Chancellery gardens. On April 20, his fifty-sixth birthday, he went up into the Chancellery building itself for a celebration—if that was the word for it.

Only a few people were present. Among them were Goering and Himmler (their dismissal from office and the Nazi Party was just hours away). The "celebration" marked their final visit with the Fuehrer. Several toasts were proposed. Hitler shook hands with all his guests. The Chancellery building, totally abandoned, was echoing and cold. The Russians were now well inside Berlin, fighting their way from street to street; the sounds of the war could be clearly heard. Within an hour, Hitler returned to the bunker.

And so ended the final observance of his birthday. April 20 had been a national holiday since 1933.

Two days later, Hitler suffered some kind of emotional breakdown. It came during a conference with his staff and senior generals. Suddenly, the understanding that the Russians were only blocks away and that the Allies couldn't be stopped on any front proved too much for him. He flew into a rage. Then he fell back into his chair, his face going from purple to chalky white to purple again. For the first time, he screamed the admission that the war was lost. He said that he would give up his command and take his life. The watching men thought he was suffering a stroke. The outburst lasted throughout the afternoon. Finally, Goebbels' quiet voice was able to calm what was left of the Fuehrer.

The episode may have been a passing phenomenon. But not Hitler's determination to commit suicide. He knew that Mussolini, when captured, had been shot in the back and then hanged

head-down from a lamppost. He wanted no such fate for himself
if captured alive nor did he want the vengeful Russians to muti-
late his body were he found dead. He told Albert Speer, who
had headed Germany's war production, that he and Eva Braun
would take their lives and that he had left orders for their
corpses to be burned. He also told Speer that he planned to
shoot his dog; actually, a few days later, the animal was taken
into a lavatory where two men—a doctor and a dog trainer—
forced a poison capsule down its throat.

By April 29, the Russians were within two or three blocks
of the bunker. The end was at hand. Only scant days—perhaps
just hours—remained until the Third Reich, which was to have
endured for a thousand years, became a charred memory. Hitler
began the day by walking with Eva Braun to a small conference
room at a moment or so after midnight. Waiting for him there
were Goebbels and Martin Bormann; Bormann had served as
Hitler's secretary and deputy leader of the Nazi Party since
Rudolf Hess' flight to Scotland. With them stood a man named
Walter Wagner.

Wagner was a minor Berlin official who had been summoned
to the bunker because he was empowered to perform weddings.
Awestruck at being in the presence of his Fuehrer, he read
the brief marriage ceremony and declared Hitler and Eva to
be man and wife. The bride wore a black taffeta dress; it seemed
more suited for a funeral (and so perhaps was appropriate)
and, of all her outfits, it was Hitler's favorite. A brief reception
was held in a nearby room. The couple ate sandwiches and
was toasted by Hitler's staff. Wagner sipped a glass of cham-
pagne and then departed for his own shelter a few streets away.
He was shot dead by a Russian soldier as he made his way
through the ruins.

Hitler and Eva retired to their suite of rooms. There, Hitler
made out his last will and testament, a document in which
his lifelong hatred of the Jews was voiced for a final time; in

it, with all his blindness of old, he blamed them for the devastation that had been wrought on Germany and Europe. The Fuehrer then worked throughout the day of the 29th with his staff.

In the afternoon of April 30, Hitler and Eva met with his staff in the corridor outside their suite. There were twenty people present, equally divided between men and women. Quiet good-byes were said. Hitler shook hands with several of the men. Then he opened the door to the suite and stood aside as Eva entered. He followed her. The door closed.

Knowing what was to come, the people stood where they were in the corridor. No one spoke as they waited for the sound of gunshots. Virtually all accounts of Hitler's death say that, in a few moments, a single gunshot was heard on the other side of the door. Author James P. O'Donnell, however, after interviewing a number of the eyewitnesses for his book, *The Bunker*, says that only silence greeted the listeners. The door to the Hitler suite was heavy and soundproof. The people waited for several minutes and then, by unspoken agreement, pushed the door open.

They found Eva and Hitler seated on a small sofa in the living room. Eva, with her feet tucked up comfortably beneath her, was seated at one end. Hitler was slumped at the other. Both were dead. Eva had taken a poison capsule. Hitler had shot himself in his right temple with a small pistol and had bitten down on a poison capsule in the same instant. The pistol lay on the floor below his outstretched arm.

It was about three o'clock in the afternoon.

The bodies were almost immediately carried up a flight of stairs to an emergency exit and into the Chancellery garden. They were placed side by side on the ground, about three yards away from the exit, which was a large square of concrete with a metal door in it. Hitler's body, covered with blood, had been wrapped in a blanket.

Goebbels and Martin Bormann accompanied the bodies. With them were an army colonel and perhaps two or three soldiers.

The men drenched the bodies with gasoline that, in accordance with Hitler's orders, had been brought to the garden the previous day. The streets around the Chancellery building were being shelled by the advancing Russians and so Goebbels hurried the funeral party back into the shelter of the emergency exit. Someone doused a large rag with gasoline, set it afire, and tossed it out at the two figures. Instantly, they were afire . . .

In just eight days from this moment—on May 7, 1945—the Third Reich would end in Germany's surrender to the Allies by Admiral Karl Donitz, who would be serving in Hitler's place as head of state. Before that day, Goebbels' wife, Magda, would kill her six children; then she and her husband would take their lives. By the end of May, Himmler would be dead of self-administered poison. In the years to come, 200 survivors of those who had built the Third Reich and fostered its horrors would be tried as war criminals; Rudolf Hess and others would be sentenced to prison, while the architects of the Jewish "final solution"—Julius Streicher, Alfred Rosenberg, Hans Frank, and Wilhelm Frick—would be sent to the gallows. Hermann Goering would also be sentenced to death, but he would cheat the hangman by swallowing poison. Finally, out of all the chaos, a new Germany would emerge, a Germany divided into two nations, one a democracy, the other a Communist satellite . . .

But now, the flames gathered about the two bodies. Smoke rose from the Chancellery garden and quickly lost itself in the blackened sky. The guns were very close.

216

RECOMMENDED READING LIST

There are literally hundreds of books on Adolf Hitler and Nazi Germany. The following should prove particularly interesting and valuable to any young reader who wishes to look further into the life of the German dictator and the tumultuous history of his Third Reich.

Bullock, Alan, *Hitler: A Study in Tyranny*. New York: Bantam, 1961.

Churchill, Winston, *The Second World War* (6 vols.). Boston: Houghton Mifflin, 1948–1953.

Douglas-Hamilton, James, *Motive for a Mission*. London: Macmillan, 1971.

Fest, Joachim C., *The Face of the Third Reich*. New York: Pantheon Books, 1970.

—— *Hitler*. New York: Random House, 1975.

Forman, James, *The White Crow*, New York: Farrar. Straus and Giroux, 1976.

Goebbels, Paul Joseph, *The Early Goebbels Diaries*. London: Weidenfeld and Nicholson, 1962.

———— H. R. Roper, ed. *The Goebbels Diaries: The Last Days*. London: Pan Books, 1979.

Hitler, Adolf, *Mein Kampf*. Boston: Houghton Mifflin, 1943.

Jenks, William A., *Vienna and the Young Hitler*. New York: Columbia University Press, 1972.

Kubizek, August, *The Young Hitler I Knew*. Boston: Houghton Mifflin, 1955.

O'Donnell, James P., *The Bunker*. Boston: Houghton Mifflin, 1978.

Phillips, Peter, *The Tragedy of Nazi Germany*. New York: Praeger, 1969.

Roper, H. R., *The Last Days of Hitler*. New York: Macmillan, 1947.

Shirer, William L., *Berlin Diary*. New York: Alfred A. Knopf, 1941.

———— *The Rise and Fall of the Third Reich*. New York: Simon and Schuster, 1960.

Speer, Albert, *Inside the Third Reich*. New York: Macmillan, 1970.

Stein, George H., ed. *Hitler*. Englewood Cliffs, New Jersey: Prentice-Hall, 1968.

Toland, John, *Adolf Hitler* (2 vols.). New York: Doubleday, 1976.

Wolfe, Burton H., *Hitler and the Nazis*. New York: G. P. Putnam's Sons, 1970.

INDEX

Academy of Arts (Vienna), 13–15
Adolf Hitler, 53
Agricultural output, 147
Air force, German. *See* Luftwaffe
Allied nations, 31, 40–41, 190; Dunkirk rescue operations by, 194–95; Europe retaken from Nazis by, 207–11, 216; loans to Germany after World War I by, 83, 91; Versailles treaty and, 45, 62–63. *See also* France; Great Britain; Russia; United States
Anschluss, 23, 179–81
Anti-Semitism of Hitler: expressed in *Mein Kampf,* 27–29, 38–39, 78; Hess and Goering attracted to, 64–65; in last will and testament, 215; promotion to regimental education officer and, 47; World War I experiences and, 38–40. *See also* Jews
Appeasement policy, 183–85

Architecture, 15, 147, 204
Aryans, 79–80. *See also* Master race concept
Astrology, 205, 211
Atom bomb, 135
Aushwitz, 131, 164–65, 172
Austria, 1, 21–24, 75–76; Bavarian plans to link with, 50, 65; Hitler's intentions toward, outlined in *Mein Kampf,* 80; invaded by Nazi Germany, 158, 179–82; World War I and, 31, 37, 40
Austria-Hungary, 22–24, 31
Austrian Customs Service, 3–4, 7
Austro-Prussian War, 22
Autobahn system, 147
Automobile industry, 146
Axis powers, 186

Baltic Sea, 185
Battle of Britain, 200, 206

Battle of the Bulge, 209
Bavaria: Austria and, 50, 65; seizure of power attempted by Nazi Party in, 65–76; post-World War I conditions in, 44–45; Weimar Republic opposed in, 46–47. *See also* Munich
BBC, 188
Beer Hall Putsch (uprising), 76, 82–83, 154
Belgium, 32, 159, 192–93, 195, 209
Belsec, 131
Benes, President Eduard, 182–83
Berchtesgaden, 178
Berghof, 178–80, 204, 211
Berlin, 99, 121, 172, 176–77; bombing of, 199, 210; Communist Party headquarters raided in, 104; conditions in, after World War I, 44–45; Hitler's bunker in, 210–15; Hitler's headquarters in, 202, 204, 211; Jewish district terrorized in, 154; Kroll Opera House in, 111; Nazi torchlight parade in, 101–102; Reichstag fire in, 104–109; Sachsenhausen (concentration camp) near, 130; World War I and, 36, 38, 40
Bible, the, 150
Blitzkrieg (lightning war), 189–90, 192
Block, Dr. Edward, 15–17
Blondi, 128, 214
Blood oath, 136, 145–46
Blood purge, 117–22
Bolivian army, 87
Bolsheviks, 39
Book burnings, 134–35
Bormann, Martin, 214, 216
Braun, Eva, 178–79, 204; in the bunker with Hitler, 212, 214–15; death of, 215–16
Braunau, 3, 5
Bredlow, General Kurt von, 120–21
British Navy, 198
Brown Shirts. *See* Storm Troopers (SA)
Bruning, Charles, 93, 96
Brunswick, 96

Buchenwald, 130, 167
Buergerbraukeller, 66–71, 73, 76
Building construction, 146–47
Bulgarians, 22
Bund Deutscher Maedel (League of German Maidens), 145
Bunker, The, 215
Buzz bomb, 209

Capitalism, 50, 55, 91
Catholic Center Party, 93, 110
Catholic Church, 1, 5–6, 148–51
Central Powers, 31
Chamberlain, Neville, 181–85, 188; Stalin plan rejected by, 187
Churchill, Prime Minister Winston, 187, 197
Clergy, 148–49
Communists, 81, 84; accused by Nazis to be Russian revolutionaries, 104–106, 108–10; in Germany after World War I, 44, 49, 54, 61; Hitler's hatred of, 40, 94, 201; Hitler's stance with wealthy industrialists against, 92; Jews arrested as, 151; killed in resettlement murders, 162; represented in German parliament, 95, 110; terror tactics used against, 104, 112, 114
Compiègne, 196
Concentration camps: atrocities against and extermination of Jews carried out in, 158–59, 163–72; clergy sent to, 148–49; development, locations, and uses of, 129–31
Condor Legion, 176–77
Conscription, 175
Construction, 146–47
Cooper, James Fenimore, 6
Croatians, 22
Crystal Night, 154–58, 181
Culture, 133–35
Czechoslovakia, 22, 158, 201; Munich Conference and, 184–85; prisoners from, in concentration camps, 166;

Sudetenland turned over to Hitler by, 182–84, 189

Dachau, 130, 149, 168
Daladier, President Edouard, 183
Danzig, 185–88
DAP. *See* German Workers Party (DAP)
Democracy, 49, 110, 216; in Spain, 176–77; unfamiliar to the German people, 127
Denmark, 191–92
Depression, economic, 91–93
Der Gifpilz (The Poisonous Mushroom), 136
Deutsche Arbeiterpartei (German Workers Party). *See* German Workers Party (DAP)
Deutschland uber Alles (Germany over all), 23
Donitz, Admiral Karl, 216
Dortmund, 153–54
Drexler, Anton, 50–52, 59
Dubno, 160–62
Dunkirk, 194–95, 199

East Prussia, 185, 208
Ebert, Friedrich, 44–45
Education system, 135–36, 145–46
Eichmann, Adolf, 159
Einsatzgruppen (Special Action Groups), 160, 162, 172
Einstein, Albert, 135
Eisner, Kurt, 44
Enabling act, 111–13, 124
England. *See* Great Britain
English Channel, 193, 207
Extermination programs: gas chambers, 163–66; gas vans, 163; resettlement murders, 160–63

Films, 133–34
First Reich, 113
Foreign trade, 152–53
France, 134, 158, 207; armistice pact signed with Nazis by, 196–97;

Czechoslovakia defense treaty with, 182–83; German defiance of Versailles treaty terms allowed by, 174–77, 181–83; Hitler's intentions toward, outlined in *Mein Kampf,* 81; Maginot Line reinforced by, 191; Mussolini and, 200; prisoners from, in concentration camps, 166–67; Prussia and, 23–24; Ruhr district and, 62–63, 92; Stalin plan rejected by, 186–87; Versailles treaty terms and, 45, 62–63; war against Nazi Germany entered by, 190–91; in World War I, 31–32, 37, 39; World War II battles fought by, 193–96. *See also* Allied nations
Francis Ferdinand, Archduke of Austria, 31
Franco, Generalissimo Francisco, 176–77
Franco-Prussian war, 23–24, 45
Frank, Hans, 159, 216
Freud, Sigmund, 134
Frick, Wilhelm, 159, 216
Fuehrer concept, 79, 114

Gas chambers, 163–66
Gas vans, 163
Geheime Staatpolizei (secret state police), 129, 154
German air force. *See* Luftwaffe
German army (the Reichswehr): support given Hitler by, 123–25; Weimar Republic opposed by, 46–49, 53, 58
German Austrians, 22–24
German Confederation, 21–22
German mark, 46, 62–63
German parliament. *See* Reichstag (national parliament)
German Workers Party (DAP): joined and taken over by Hitler, 51–59; renamed, 59–60; spied on by Hitler, 49–50. *See also* Nazi Party
Germany, 5, 11–12, 22–24, 29, 83; Allied forces' penetration of, 209–11,

Germany *(Continued)*
213–16; Austria invaded by, 179–82; conditions contributing to Hitler's rise to power in, 61–63, 126–31, 171–72; conscription announced in, 175; Crystal Night in, 154–58; Czechoslovakia taken over by, 182–85; economic depression in, 91–93; forceful seizure of power from Bavarian government attempted by Nazi Party in, 65–76; Great Britain and France at war against, 188, 190–91; Hitler appointed Chancellor of, 99–102; Hitler's plans for, outlined in *Mein Kampf*, 78–81 *(see also Mein Kampf)*; Jews enslaved, tortured, and exterminated in, 158–72; League of Nations and, 174; military strength rebuilt in, 173–77; Nazi Party outlawed, then rebuilt in, 82–87, 90 *(see also* Nazi Party); North African campaign of, 200–201, 207; Poland invaded by, 185–88; post-World War I conditions in, 43–47; Reichstag taken under Nazi control in, 102–15; Rhineland retaken by, 175–77; Russian campaign of, 201–203, 206–207; social and economic sanctions against Jews imposed in, 97, 151–54; Spanish Civil War and, 176–77; supreme authority achieved by Hitler in, 123–26; Sweden unmolested by, 191–92; Twilight War and, 191–92; United States at war with, 203, 207, 209; Versailles treaty terms for, 45–46 *(see also* Versailles peace treaty); war strategies in Europe of, 190–200; wealthy industrialists' support of Nazi Party in, 92, 103; World War I role of, 31–39. *See also* Hitler, Adolf; Third Reich; Weimar Republic
Gestapo, 129, 154
Giesing, Dr. Erwin, 212
Goebbels, Magda, 210, 216

Goebbels, Paul Joseph, 95; background of, 85; blood purge and, 118, 120; bunker occupied with Hitler by, 210–11, 213–16; Crystal Night of violence ordered by, 154–58; Polish invasion reinterpreted to German people by, 187–88; propaganda as used by, 85, 102–104, 110, 124–25, 128, 187–88; Reich Chamber of Culture established by, 133; Reichstag fire and, 108; suicide of, 216; torchlight parade in Berlin arranged by, 101–102, 113
Goering, Hermann, 85, 131; background of, 64–65; Crystal Night and, 157–58; in final days of Third Reich, 210, 213; forceful seizure of Bavarian government attempted by Nazi Party and, 70, 72–76; Gestapo administered by, 129; League of Air Sports organized by, 174; Morell called "Master of the Imperial Needle" by, 206; Nazi Party blood purge and, 120–21; Nazi Party campaign for majority Reichstag representation and, 104, 110; Reichstag fire and, 105, 107–108; Roehm and, 117; suicide of, 216; terror tactics used against political opposition by, 114; in World War II, 190, 193–94, 196, 198, 209
Graf, Ulrich, 74
Great Britain, 134; appeasement policy followed by, 183–85; bombed by Germany, 197–200, 209; German defiance of Versailles treaty terms allowed by, 174–77, 181–82; loans to Germany made by, 83, 91; Stalin plan rejected by, 186–87; war against Germany declared by, 188, 190–91; war against Japan declared by, 203; World War I and, 31, 37; World War II battles fought by, 193–95. *See also* Allied nations
Greece, 200
Grynszpan, Herschel, 154

Guernica, 177
Gutmann, Lieutenant Hugo, 39
Gypsy prisoners, 168, 170

Hamburg, 97
Hanisch, Reinhold, 19–20
Hanslbauer Hotel, 118
Hawaii, 203
Heine, Heinrich, 134
Hess, Rudolph, 85, 102, 196; background of, 64; flight to Scotland of, 205, 214; in forceful seizure of Bavarian government attempted by Nazi Party, 72, 74–76; German court system and, 132; *Mein Kampf* dedicated to, 78; sentenced to prison, 216
Heydrich, Reinhard, 129; Crystal Night and, 155–56; extermination programs supervised by, 159
Hiedler, Johann Georg, 2, 4
Highway construction, 146–47
Himmler, Heinrich, 102; astrology and, 205; background of, 85–86; Crystal Night and, 157; extermination programs supervised by, 159, 163, 167–68; in final days of Third Reich, 209–10, 213; murder of Geli Raubel suspected of, 90; Roehm and, 117; SS commanded by, 86, 128; suicide of, 216
Hindemith, Paul, 133
Hindenberg, Field Marshal Paul von, 116–17, 122; death of, 123–25; escalating powers granted to Hitler by, 108–109, 113; Hitler appointed Chancellor by, 99–100; Hitler opposed by, 92–96, 98; Reichstag dissolved by, for special elections, 103
Hindenberg, Major Oskar von, 99, 125
Hitler, Adolf: anti-Semitism of, 27–29, 38–40, 47, 64–65, 78, 214–15; appointed Chancellor, 99–102; astrology and, 205, 211; atrocities against and extermination of Jews by, 158–

72; Austria invaded by, 179–82; *Blitzkrieg* style of warfare introduced by, 189–90; Britain bombed by, 197–200, 209; childhood of, 5–13; combat experience of, 32–37; and death of his mother, 15–17; defeated as presidential candidate, 95–96; court system under control of, 131–32; Crystal Night and, 154–58; culture of Germany under control of, 133–35; depressions suffered by, 72, 90, 128, 206, 212; early political thinking of, 21, 24–26; early speeches of, 54–59; education system under control of, 135–46; European territory taken by, 190–97; Eva Braun and, 178–79, 204, 214–16; family history of, 1–5; final days of, 210–16; forceful seizure of Bavarian government attempted by, 65–76; Geli Raubel and, 88–90; as German army education officer, 47–48; German Workers Party taken over by, 49–50; Great Britain and France enter war against, 188, 190–91; at home for destitute men, 19–21, 24; July Plot against, 208–209; marriage of, 179, 214; medications taken by, 206, 212; *Mein Kampf* written by, 78 (*see also Mein Kampf*); military strength of Germany rebuilt by, 173–77; Munich agreement violated by, 184; Nazi Party blood purge and, 115–22; Nazi Party created by, 53–60; Nazi Party rebuilt by, 82–87, 90; North African campaign of, 200–201, 207; pageantry as used by, 57–58; Poland invaded by, 185–88; political ambitions formed by, 42–46; political events surrounding early life of, 21–24; in prison for treason, 76–78; reasons for rise to power of, 126–31, 171–72; Reichstag taken under control of, 102–15; religious institutions and, 147–51; and Roehm, split

Hitler *(Continued)*
over use of SA, 87, 115–16; Russia attacked by, 201–203, 206–207; sanity of, collapsing, 128, 206, 208–209, 211, 213; schooling of, 7–10, 14–15, 17–18; social and economic sanctions against Jews imposed by, 151–54; Stalin and, 186–87, 190, 201; Sudentenland gained by, 182–84; suicide of, 214–15; supreme authority in Germany achieved by, 123–26; terror tactics used against political opposition by, 104, 109–10, 112, 114–15; United States at war with, 203, 207, 209; Weimar Republic declared at an end by, 113; women and, 11–12, 77, 88–90, 178–79; workers under control of, 146–47; World War I and, 30–42. *See also* Germany; Third Reich

Hitler, Alois, 1–4, 7–10
Hitler, Alois, Jr., 2–3, 5–7
Hitler, Angela, 3, 5, 7, 12–13, 87–88
Hitler, Edmond, 5
Hitler, Gustav, 4
Hitler, Ida, 4
Hitler, Klara Poelzl. *See* Poelzl, Klara
Hitler, Otto, 4
Hitler, Paula, 5, 12–13, 15–17
Hitler Youth Movement, 135–36, 145–46, 174
Holland, 158
Holy Roman Empire of German States, 21, 113, 127, 182
Homosexuality, 116
Hungary, 22–24, 80

I. G. Farben chemical works, 164
Indo-China, 203
Inflation, 62–64, 91
Inside the Third Reich, 178
Iron Cross, 33–34, 39
Iron ore, 191–92
Italy, 184, 207; North African campaign and, 200; Pact of Steel signed by, 186, 188; World War I and, 31

Jansten, Stephanie, 11–12, 88
Japan, 203, 207
Jews: abused in or excluded from German schools, 135–36, 151–52; artistic works of, banned, 133–35; atrocities against and systematic murder of, 158–72; banned from teaching, 135; Christian European prejudice against, 26–27; clergy imprisoned for defense of, 149; Crystal Night of violence against, 154–58; depression blamed by Hitler on, 91; deserted by Germans in fear of the SA, 97; economic and social sanctions against, 133–34, 151–54; extermination programs directed against, 160–66; in the German army in World War I, 39; Hitler's plans for, outlined in *Mein Kampf*, 79–80; marriage or sexual intercourse with, forbidden, 152, 156; reasons for failure to resist Nazi persecution, 171–72; slave labor forced from, 130, 164, 166–67; in Vienna, 181. *See also* Anti-Semitism of Hitler
July Plot, 208–209
Jungmaedel (Young Maidens) program, 136
Jungvolk (Young Folk) program, 136, 145

Kahr, Gustav von, 65–72, 121
Kaiser Wilhelm II, 32, 40–42, 44, 46
Kantzow, Carin von, 65
Kirdorf, Emil, 92
Kroll Opera House, 111–13
Krupp munitions factory, 164
Kubizek, August, 11; on the death of Hitler's mother, 16–17; Hitler's Vienna years remembered by, 18–19, 29

Labor camps, 130–31
Labor unions, 92, 114, 146
Land reforms, 147

Index

Landsberg, 77, 82–83, 87, 121, 128
League of Nations, 174
Lebensraum plan, 136, 158–59, 201; outlined in *Mein Kampf,* 80–81
Legal system, 131–33
Leisure time, 147
Leningrad, 201
Leopold III, King of Belgium, 193
Leopoldstat, 29
Linz, 7–8, 11, 15–18; concentration camp near, 131
Literature, 133–35
London, 199
London, Jack, 134
Lossow, General Otto von, 65–72
Ludendorff, General Erich von, 53, 63, 92; cultivated by Hitler, 58; and Nazi Party attempt to seize Bavarian government, 69–76; 1918 German offensive led by, 47
Luftwaffe (German air force), 174, 181, 190, 193–94; RAF and, 198–200

Madagascar, island of, 159
Magazines, 133
Maginot, Line, 191, 193, 195
Magyars, 22
Mann, Thomas, 134, 135
Mannerheim, the, 19–21, 24, 29, 48
Master race concept, 79–80; Himmler and, 86; taught in German schools, 135
Matzelsberger, Franziska, 3–4
Mauthausen, 131, 167
Mecklenberg, 130
Medical experiments, 167–70
Mein Kampf (My Struggle), 8, 14, 197; anti-Semitism expressed in, 27–29, 38–39, 78; Bible to be replaced by, 149–50; on the death of Hitler's mother, 17; *Fuehrer* concept in, 114; on the German Workers Party, 52; Hitler's master plan outlined in, 78–81; *Lebensraum* plan in, 80–81, 173, 201; on political ambitions, 42–

43, 47; on World War I, 31, 38–39, 41; the writing of, 77–78
Mendelssohn, Felix, 133
Milch, Erhard, 92
Military Cross, 33
Money value, 62–64, 91
Morell, Dr. Theodor, 205–206, 212
Moscow, 201–202
Mueller, Ludwig, 149
Mueller, Professor Karl von, 47–48
Munich, 77, 95, 154, 210; anti-Republican activity in, 46–53; art museum planned by Hitler for, 204; blood purge arrests and killings near, 118–19, 121; Dachau near, 130; German Workers Party taken over by Hitler in, 53–60; Goering in, 65; Hitler and Geli Raubel in, 88, 90, 92; Hitler's early years in, 29–30, 32; Hitler's villa outside, 178; Nazi Party seizure of Bavarian government attempted in, 66–79; post-World War I conditions in, 43–45; synagogues burned in, 153–54
Munich Conference, 184–85
Music, 133
Mussolini, Benito, 184, 200; death of, 214; Pact of Steel and, 186

Napoleon, 21, 197
National Socialist German Workers Party *(Nationalsozialistiche Deutsche Arbeiterpartei).* See Nazi Party
National Socialist Teachers' League, 135
Nazi flag, 57–58, 102
Nazi Party, 9, 53; blood purge carried out within, 115–22; Crystal Night and, 157; forceful seizure of Bavarian government attempted by, 65–74; majority representation in Reichstag sought by, 102–11; origin of, 59–60 (*see also* German Workers Party); outlawed, 82; rebuilt, 83–87, 90; supported by wealthy industri-

225

Nazi Party *(Continued)*
alists, 92, 103. *See also* Hitler, Adolf; Third Reich
Nazi salute, 102
Netherlands, the, 192–93
Neumann, Josef, 19–20
Newspapers, 133
Niemoeller, Reverend Martin, 149
Normandy, 207
North African campaign, 200–201, 207, 209
North Sea, 191–92
Norway, 191–92
Nuremberg, 153–54

O'Donnell, James P., 215
Oil, 200–201, 206
Operation Barbarossa, 201–202
Operation Dynamo, 194–95
Operation Sea Lion, 198–200
Oslo, 192

Pact of Steel, 186, 188
Panzer (tank) divisions, 201, 209
Paris, 39, 195–96
Pasewalk, 37
Pearl Harbor, 203
Poelzl, Klara, 1, 3–10, 13, 18; death of, 15–17
Poetsch, Dr. Leopold, 9
Poincaré, French President Raymond, 62
Poland, 185–87, 201; *Blitzkrieg* style of warfare in, 189; concentration camps in, 131; extermination programs in, 162–64; Hitler's plan for, 80, 158–59; invaded by Hitler, 185–88; prisoners from, in concentration camps, 166, 169
Polish Corridor, 185–87
Pope Pius XI, 148
Propaganda: Goebbels' use of, 85, 102–104, 110, 124–25; Hitler's early views on, 25; media used for, 133. *See also* Radio broadcasts
Prostitution, 29, 167

Protestant churches, 148–51
Proust, Marcel, 134
Prussia, 22–24

Quisling, Major Vidkun, 192

"Racial science," 135
Radar, 198
Radio broadcasts, 103–104, 110, 125; Polish invasion and, 133
Rascher, Dr. Sigmund, 168–70
Raubel, Angela Maria (Geli), 88–90, 92, 178–79
Raubel, Leo, 88
Ravensbruek, 130–131
Realschule, 27, 131
Recreation programs, 147
Reich Church, 148–49
Reichstag (national parliament), 84; enabling act passed by, 111–13, 124; fire in building housing, 104–109; majority representation in, sought by Nazi Party, 102–11; rivalries within, 93, 96; terror tactics used by Nazi Party against opposition in, 112, 114–15
Reichswehr. *See* German army (the Reichswehr)
Religious institutions, 147–51
Remarque, Erich Maria, 134, 135
Rhineland, 175–77, 181–82
Rise and Fall of the Third Reich, The, 15, 20, 146
Roehm, Ernst, 128; in attempted Nazi Party seizure of the Bavarian government, 64, 66, 70–75; blood purge carried out against, 117–20, 123, 130; and Hitler, split over use of SA, 87, 115–16; Storm Troopers organized by, 55–57, 59
Roman Catholic Church, 1, 5–6, 148–51
Rommel, General Erwin, 201, 209
Rosenberg, Alfred, 159, 216
Rostov, 201–202
Rotterdam, 193

Index

Royal Air Force (RAF), 198–200
Ruhr district, 62–63, 92
Rumania, 201
Russia, 186; Czechoslovakia defense treaty with, 182–83; German forces overcome by, 208–11, 213–16; Hitler's plan for, 80–81, 158–59; invaded by Germany, 201–203, 206–207; nonaggression pact with Nazi Germany signed by, 187; Polish territory claimed by, 190; prisoners from, in concentration camps, 166, 168–70; resettlement murders in, 160–62; World War I and, 31, 39–41

SA. *See* Storm Troopers (SA)
Sachsenhausen, 130
Scheubner-Richter, Max, 74–76
Schicklgruber, Anna, 2–3
Schleicher, General Kurt von, 96, 98, 116, 120
Schmidt, Maria, 7
Schuschnigg, Kurt von, 180
SD (*Sicherheidienst*, security service), 129, 154–58
2nd Bavarian Infantry Regiment, 32
Second Reich, 113
Seisser, Colonel Hans von, 65–72
Serbia, 22, 31
Service Medal, 33
Shirer, William L., 15, 20; on atrocities by German medical men, 168; on Hitler at Compiègne, 196; on the Hitler Youth Movement, 145–46
Shutzstaffel. *See* SS
Sicherheidienst. *See* SD
Siegfried Line, 176
16th Bavarian Reserve Infantry Regiment, 32
Slave labor, 80, 130, 159, 166–67; German industries run on, 164
Slavic peoples, 22–24; half to be enslaved, half to be killed, 159; Hitler's plans for, outlined in *Mein Kampf*, 79–80; in Poland, 185

Social Democratic Party, 40; dubbed "the November criminals," 42, 46, 56, 1933 election showing of, 110; terror tactics used against, 112, 114
Socialism, 92; German Workers Party and, 49, 55, 57
Sonderkommandos, 165–66
Spain, 176–77
Speer, Albert, 178, 214
Spital, 1–3, 7
Spitfires, 200
Sports, 147, 174
SS (*Shutzstaffel*, guard detachment), 188, 210; concentration camps run by, 130; Crystal Night carried out by, 154–58; developed by Himmler, 86; functions of, 128–29; Nazi Party blood purge and, 119; resettlement murders carried out by, 160–62
Stadelheim Prison, 118–19
Stalin, Joseph, 201; alliance with France and Great Britain attempted by, 186; nonaggression pact with Hitler signed by, 187; Polish territory claimed by, 190
Stalingrad, 206
Stauffenberg, Colonel Klaus von, 208–209
Steyr, 10–13, 15
Storm Troopers (SA), 56–57, 63, 128; in clashes with Communists, 94, 96–97; concentration camps initially run by, 130; Crystal Night carried out by, 155–58; in seizure of Bavarian government attempted by Hitler, 66–75; Hitler and Roehm split over use of, 87, 115–16; origin and growth of, 56–57, 59, 86; terror tactics used against political opposition by, 104, 109–10, 112, 114–15; Viennese Jews brutalized by, 181. *See also* SS (*Shutzstaffel*, guard detachment)
Strasser, Gregor, 84–85, 121

227

Streicher, Julius, 159, 216
Sturmabteilung (Storm Detachment). *See* Storm Troopers (SA)
Sudetenland, 182–84, 188
Suez Canal, 201
Swastika, 110, 196; Christian cross to be replaced by, 149–50; symbolic meaning of, 57–58
Sweden: Goering in, 64–65, 75–76; unmolested by Germany, 191
Synagogues, 153–56

Tanks, 189, 192, 201
Thaelman, Ernst, 95
Theater, 133
Third Reich: court system in, 131–33; culture in, 133–35; education in, 135–36, 145–46; final days of, 210–16; foreign trade interests of, 152–53; meaning of name given, 113; plot against Hitler by officers of, 208–209; religious institutions in, 147–51; workers in, 146–47 *See also* Germany; Hitler, Adolf
Thyssen, Fritz, 92
Toland, John, 53
Treblinka, 130
Twilight War, 191–92

Ukraine, 160–62
United Nations, 174
United States, 134; loans made to Germany by, 83, 91; stock market crash in, 91; World War I and, 31, 40; World War II and, 203, 207. *See also* Allied nations
University of Berlin, 134
University of Munich, 47, 64, 86

Van der Lubbe, Marinus, 105–107
Vatican, the, 148

Vernichtungslager (extermination camps), 164–166. *See also* Extermination programs
Versailles peace treaty, 45, 81, 115, 124; Germany humiliated by, 127; Nazi defiance of terms of, 146, 173–77, 179; Polish Corridor and, 186
Vienna, 3–4, 13, 55, 88–89, 95; anti-Semitism developed during Hitler's years in, 27–29; Hitler an aspiring artist in, 14–21, 30; Hitler a street wanderer in, 18–19; Jews in, brutalized, 181; political strategies developed by Hitler in, 25, 43, 58, 66, 128
Volkisher Beobachter, 57
Volkswagen, 147
Vom Rath, Ernst, 154
Von Papen, Franz, 96

Wagner, Richard, 11
Wagner, Walter, 214
War Ministry, 66, 70–75
Warsaw, 162–63, 171, 190
Weimar, 45, 130
Weimar Republic: cancellation of rights granted by constitution of, 109; end of, proclaimed by Hitler, 113; formation of, 45; internal opposition to, 46–49, 53, 58, 61; political and economic problems faced by, 61–64
Wells, H. G., 134
West Berlin, 107
Wilhelm, Kaiser, 31
Wilhelm II, Kaiser, 32, 40–42, 44, 46
World War I, 30–42, 203

Ypres, 32, 34
Yugoslavia, 200

Zhukov, General Georgi, 202–203
Zola, Emile, 134

EDWARD F. DOLAN, JR., a fourth-generation Californian, now lives just north of San Francisco. A full-time writer of non-fiction books, he worked for many years as a newspaperman and magazine editor.

He began writing books in 1958 and his first, *Pasteur and the Invisible Giants*, was published by Dodd, Mead & Company. Since then, he has written more than forty books for young people and adults. His titles include three histories of exploration and seventeen biographies. He has also written numerous magazine articles and short stories. His most recent biography is *Matthew Henson, Black Explorer*.

Mr. Dolan and his wife, Rose, have two children, both grown and married.